High Realism in Canada

High Realism in Canada

Paul Duval

Clarke, Irwin & Company Limited
Toronto   Vancouver

ISBN 0-7720-0697-0

PRINTED IN CANADA

12345 SM 77 76 75 74

Contents

Acknowledgements

Among those whose co-operation helped to make this book possible are: Mr. T.R. MacDonald, Director, Art Gallery of Hamilton; Mr. David Carter, Director, Montreal Museum of Fine Arts; Mr. John Climer, Director, Mendel Art Gallery, Saskatoon; Miss Jean Boggs, Director, National Gallery of Canada; and Dr. Michael Pflug, Toronto.

The following private art galleries and dealers were also very helpful: Mr. Walter Moos, Gallery Moos, Toronto; Mr. Jerrold Morris, The Morris Gallery, Toronto; Mr. Jack Wildridge, Roberts Gallery, Toronto; Dr. Max Stern, The Dominion Gallery, Montreal; Mrs. Mira Godard, Marlborough Godard Gallery, Toronto; Mrs. Nancy Poole, Nancy Poole Gallery, London and Toronto; Mrs. B. Dunkleman, The Dunkleman Gallery, Toronto: Mr. Simon Dresdnere, Gallery Dresdnere, Toronto; and Fischer Fine Arts Ltd., London, England.

To the many private owners of works reproduced in this book, some of whom wished to remain anonymous, I owe very special thanks.

Finally, a warm acknowledgement goes to all those artists whose works are reproduced here, and to the many people who carefully guided this book through its various stages of preparation, design and production.

Preface

"High realism" is used throughout this book to describe a special kind of pictorial art which is characterized by an intense concern and involvement with subject matter as such. The term embraces a variety of attitudes and styles (unlike "magic realism," "photographic realism" or "hyper realism," which have a more limited application). Furthermore, it is one that all of the living artists represented in this book are happy to acknowledge as applicable to their painting.

The essential qualities of high realism are objectivity of vision, sharpness of definition, precision of technique, accuracy of detail, and excellence of craftsmanship.

These are not new factors in New World art; a high realist approach has played an important role in Canadian painting for almost two hundred years. Accordingly, though this volume is primarily devoted to the art of contemporary high realists, I have included an introductory chapter dealing with those artists of the nineteenth and early twentieth century who most closely relate to the philosophy, concept and technique of today's high realists. Those who mistakenly look upon the genre as a recently emerged fashion need only take a backward glance.

Another common misconception is that high realist painting "looks just like a photograph." The people who make such an observation should look again. Though high realists use nature as their take-off point, they bring to it a highly personal vision, style and technique; they do not hesitate to vary, edit, or intensify natural form or colour. Their prime creative objective is to enable us to experience reality anew through their art.

The number of artists included in this volume has been purposely limited so that each of them may be represented by a selection of works sufficiently large to reveal his personal style and concepts. There are others who might well have been included, but I believe that these thirteen contemporary painters most eloquently illustrate the level and character of high realism in Canada today.

PAUL DUVAL

Studio Building, Toronto

The realist tradition in Canada

Those people who look upon high realism as a recent fashion in Canada only need to be guided back 175 years to see that it has a long and respectable tradition. As early as 1800 the style was introduced into this country by German and·British academy-trained painters.

Throughout most of the nineteenth century the academies of Britain, Düsseldorf and London were staffed by teachers of superb technical ability and creative dedication. Such men were disciplined artists, complete masters of their media. Canada's early realists thus had the benefit of impressive instruction. Among the nineteenth-century masters who influenced them, through direct teaching or example, were Thomas Eakins (1844-1916), Sir John Everett Millais (1829-96), Jean Léon Gérôme (1824-1904), Johann Wilhelm Schirmer (1807-63) and William Harnett (c. 1851-95).

The attitude of *caveat emptor* taken by so many casual contemporary painters was unthinkable to such masters. They not only clearly felt that they owed it to the eventual buyer of their art to give of their best, but that they owed it to themselves.

William Berczy (1744-1813) was one of the first, and among the best, of Canada's early high realists. His creative approach and completed paintings make him a true forerunner of today's realist school. Berczy is best known for his full-length portrait of the Mohawk Chief Joseph Brant (National Gallery of Canada), which could easily fit into a contemporary exhibition of high realism. The close attention to detail, crisp delineation of form, and clarity of colour in the portrait are characteristic of present-day techniques. Berczy made a practice of executing minutely rendered preparatory studies for each section of his paintings, and his notebooks contain superbly drawn details, such as the log in the foreground of the Brant portrait.

Like a number of other early Canadian realists, Berczy was German-born and trained. He studied at the Academy of Arts in Vienna, under Anton Maulbertsch and Marten van Meytens. The precise technique of these prominent academicians unquestionably gave the young artist the technical skill that remained with him throughout his career, though some of his portraits suggest that he was also influenced by the pastel and oil portraits of his German contemporary, Anton Groff (1736-1836).

Berczy's career, however, was not devoted merely to art. He was also architect, scientist, writer, and land agent. He was, in fact, one of the most colourful personalities in Canada at the turn of the eighteenth century.

He arrived in this country by accident. In 1792 he was employed by the Earl of Bath to oversee the establishment of a party of German immigrants in the United States, but was obliged to redirect the group to Canada after difficulties with American authorities. He chose to settle his charges on a tract of land near Markham, Ontario.

It is to Berczy's misadventures as a land agent that we probably owe the existence of the remarkable paintings he executed in this country. He was driven by economic necessity to paint portraits of many of Canada's prominent citizens of the period, and his studies of Joseph Brant, General Sir Isaac Brock, General Robert Prescott and Sir John Gore demonstrate that his fine training in realism serves history as well as art.

Berczy was a slow, deliberate craftsman. He not only prepared many precise pencil drawings for a painting, but spent a long time in its actual execution. His eight-figure group portrait of the Woolsey family (National Gallery of Canada) took him from the fall of 1808 to the spring of 1809 to complete. But whether he was depicting people, flowers or animals, Berczy revealed the same clear-eyed, incisive and subtle realism. His painstaking rendering of every contour succeeds in holding his subjects in a state of suspended animation for all time.

During the 1830's, a number of newly arrived topographical artists were at work in Canada. Some were in transit and others had taken up permanent residence. Among these were William Henry Bartlett (1809-54), Thomas Young (whose dates have yet to be ascertained) and James Duncan (1806-81). These three artists, while employed in making factual records, often did so in such a manner that their paintings entered the realm of creative realism.

William Bartlett, a London-born prodigy whose curiosity and industry took him to many parts of the world to record foreign scenery, was apprenticed at the age of twelve, and received a thorough training in art. His employer, John Britton, referring to young Bartlett's seven-year apprenticeship, remarked, "In the course of one year, Bartlett surpassed all of his associates and rivals in accuracy, style and rapidity." This was the training that Bartlett brought to bear when he illustrated Nathaniel Parker Willis' *Canadian Scenery* in 1838. The hundred-odd sepia watercolour drawings he created for that work possess both accuracy and charm.

Of even greater interest to the student of high realism are a number of larger canvases in oil which are sometimes attributed to Bartlett, but about which there is no positive evidence of authorship. Four of these works, in the Sigmund Samuel Collection, Royal Ontario Museum, are brilliant and compelling examples of close and original observation.

WILLIAM BERCZY *Portrait of Joseph Brant*
Oil on canvas c.1800-1807 24 x 18
National Gallery of Canada

Each painting bears the entwined monogram HB, but whether they are by Bartlett or not, they are among the most skilful and entertaining of all early records of Canada – particularly of French Canadian town life – in existence. *The Market Place, Quebec* depicts a team of exotically dressed, pigtailed acrobats performing for a circle of spectators. *The Cathedral, Montreal,* shows a tightrope-walker performing in the same setting that appears in the Bartlett view drawn for *Canadian Scenery.*

Few details have yet been uncovered about Thomas Young except the bare facts that he probably emigrated from England and was active as an architect and artist in Toronto from 1835 on. He taught drawing at Upper Canada College during the 1830's, and was an engineer for the city from 1840 until 1842. He is best known for his early views of Toronto, made familiar through the lithographic reproductions published by the American N. Currier in 1835-36.

The small, crisply delineated oil, *View of King Street, Toronto*, in the Sigmund Samuel Collection, Royal Ontario Museum, usually attributed to Young, is a good example of early high realism in Canada, regardless of its authorship.

Among the many recorders of the Canadian scene during the early Victorian years, James Duncan was one of the busiest, and one of the most original in his approach to composition. His skill as a draughtsman made it possible for him to select and accent factual detail with dramatic effect. This is all the more extraordinary in that Duncan, who arrived in Canada at the age of nineteen, appears to be self-taught.

Many of Duncan's small oils and large watercolours of Montreal scenes attest to his creative abilities, but his eye for portraying the particular is best seen in his smaller watercolour vignettes. Some of these are to be found in his sketch books, one of which, entitled *Canada*, consists of thirty-one views of Indians trading, children sleighing, and ice-cutting on the St. Lawrence.

In addition to Berczy, three other German-born or Teutonic-trained artists who brought their talents to Canada during the nineteenth century were Cornelius Krieghoff (1815-72), Otto Jacobi (1812-1901) and William Raphael (1833-1914).

Krieghoff came to Canada via the United States, and there can be little doubt that certain American painters added their influence to that of his German masters. (Althouth he was born in Amsterdam, Krieghoff studied in Germany, at the Düsseldorf school, and possibly in Rotterdam as well.) Certainly his works show characteristics of both the intensely realistic Düsseldorf Academy and those of Dutch late-eighteenth and early-nineteenth-century painting.

He arrived in New York in 1837, and it is believed that he subsequently spent time in Florida, Rochester and New England. Although it does not appear to have been noted, there is strong stylistic evidence that Krieghoff knew and was influenced by the canvases of Thomas Cole (1801-48), a founder of the American Hudson River School of landscape painting. There are striking similarities in technique, colour and composition between Cole's detailed and dramatic views of New York State and New England done during the 1820's and 1830's and those executed by Krieghoff in Quebec decades later. Cole's romantic high-realism canvases, *The Clove, Catskills* and *Kaaterskill Falls* are different from anything done in Europe at that time. Krieghoff almost certainly happened upon such paintings during his years in the United States, or later trips to New England and New York. Even Cole's themes, such as *The Last of the Mohicans*, were later adopted by Krieghoff.

Krieghoff was far from a finished painter when he arrived in Canada in the early 1840's. The paintings he executed from 1841 to 1845 lack both the authority of draughtsmanship and the richness of colour and texture which marked the works of his maturity. His later works, however, display an easy command of composition. His masterpiece, *Merrymaking* (Beaverbrook Art Gallery, Fredericton), contains more that sixty figures. It was probably the influence of Cole and other painters of the Hudson River School that resulted in such authoritative and detailed achievement.

Krieghoff's realist focus became sharpest when he portrayed close-ups of individual subjects, human or otherwise. The portrait of *John Budden; The Steamship, Quebec* and *Horse Fraser Ridden by Mr. Miller* (National Gallery of Canada), all contain elements of high realism.

Otto Jacobi, who followed in the footsteps of Krieghoff, was one of the most highly trained, technically, of the many artists who emigrated to Canada during the nineteenth century. Born in Königsberg, Prussia, he acquired his impressive command of technique during training at the Art Academies of Berlin and Düsseldorf. The style he developed at these centres evolved from the example of such teachers of realistic landscape as Johann Wilhelm Schirmer (1807-63) and Franz Anton Maulbertsch (1724-96). The landscapes of Jacobi's early career and those painted when he first came to Canada in 1860 bear a close stylistic resemblance to those of Maubertsch.

Jacobi's first trip to this country resulted from the reputation he had established early in his career. His landscapes had an appeal far beyond his native Prussia, and his canvases had a market throughout Europe, as well as in England and America. His realistic style appealed to patrons, and he was commissioned in 1860 to paint a view of Shawinigan Falls, in Quebec, as a gift for the Prince of Wales (later King Edward VII). Jacobi seems to have found Quebec to his liking, and apart from brief visits to the United States and Toronto (where he lived from 1878-79 and 1891-93), he concentrated on landscapes of the lower Ottawa Valley and the Laurentians.

During his first decade in Quebec, from 1860-70, Jacobi maintained the disciplined, sharp delineation of form which reflected his German academic background. This can be seen in such canvases as *Falls of Ste Anne, Quebec* (1865 – Art Gallery of Ontario). Later, his work dissipated into an increasingly vaporous style, with a de-emphasis on form and a markedly romantic and atmospheric character. Many of his canvases of the 1880's have the quality of watercolours – a medium which he came to favour in his later years.

William Raphael, who was born in Prussia, was a student at the Berlin Academy in 1854-55, twenty years after Jacobi had left there. He emigrated to Canada via New York in 1857, but he did not have Jacobi's background of international success, and was forced by economic necessity to teach school in Montreal and to paint portraits for most of his life.

The works for which Raphael takes a significant place in Canadian art are his detailed and affectionate human studies, such as *Immigrants at Montreal* (1866 – National Gallery of Canada), *Bonsecours Market* (1880) and *Toboganning*.

Raphael's deliberate organization of compositional elements, clarity of description, and concern for pictorial facts all relate to the high realism ethic as practised by many painters of today. Many of his tiny sketchbooks (measuring 4″ x 6″ and 5″ x 8″) still exist, supplying eloquent testimony in pen and pencil to the pains he took in collecting the minute details from which he composed his canvases in oil.

William George Richardson Hind (1833-88) was one of the most original talents in Canada's nineteenth-century painting. Many of his pictures are perfect examples of high realism. Small in size, measuring only a few inches each way, Hind's best pictures are filled with the most intricate and closely observed details. They possess the clarity of line, lucidity of colour and novelty of point of view which characterize the best of present-day realism. In a portrait of his brother, Henry Youle Hind, he utilized a close cross-hatch technique to build up his forms, the same technique which is used by many of today's egg-tempera painters. Compositionally, too, many of his designs strike a remarkably contemporary note. Such miniature oils as *Breaking a Road in*

CORNELIUS KRIEGHOFF *The Steamship Quebec*
Oil on canvas 1853 27 x 37
Collection: Dr W.R. Franks

Manitobah [sic] (8″ x 10″) and *Horse Drinking at Ice Hole* (9-1/4″ x 12-1/4″), both in the Public Archives, Ottawa, are portrayals of animals which suggest a monumentality larger than life. Their frozen, statue-like forms are sculpted in space with the permanence of an unforgettable scene caught in the niche of memory.

Hind's small landscapes, such as *View from Sunnyside,* could easily settle into place in a present-day realist exhibition. This panel offers a view of barns, fences and trees viewed beyond a silhouetted foreground of window sill. A tiny 6″x6″ self-portrait with a meerschaum pipe (B.C. Archives, Victoria) is probably Hind's masterpiece, and regardless of scale, is certainly one of the most compelling portraits ever done in this country. It is executed with a sharp focus vision and prodigious skill. The penetration of his spectacled gaze suggests the intensity with which the artist looked at nature and across time.

William Hind, born in Nottingham, England, came to Canada in 1852 and travelled extensively in this country. His work falls into two broad categories – sketches in pencil and watercolours done on the spot, and the more consciously designed and deliberate oils and watercolours worked up from them. The spontaneous records were made *en route* during a number of expeditions. The first probably took place in 1861, when Hind served as official artist for a Labrador expedition headed by his brother Henry, who was a geologist, scientist and writer. In 1862, Hind left on a second expedition westward with a band of forty-four Overlanders, bound for Fort Garry and the Cariboo country, then in the midst of gold-rush fever. He made valuable factual records during all these journeys, and worked up many of his on-the-spot notes into more complete paintings during a several-year-stay in Victoria, British Columbia.

Hind spent his last years in Sussex, New Brunswick, not too far from "Sunnyside," his brother's home at Windsor, Nova Scotia. The close relationship between William and Henry Hind must have been important to the former, who seems to have been constantly encouraged by his scientist brother.

Little is known of what formal training in art Hind may have received in England, but it must have been considerable, judging from his most finished works in oil. He probably encountered the work of such Royal Academicians as Richard Redgrave and possibly that of the Pre-Raphaelites.

There is an uncanny similarity in the style of Hind and that of R.J. Best, a Maritime painter who was working at the same time. Best's detailed landscapes of the Saint John, New Brunswick, area could easily be mistaken for those by Hind. Unfortunately, little is known about Best, and it would be impossible to say just how closely the two artists were associated, or whether Hind did indeed have a direct influence upon Best's work.

High realist tendencies are found in much early Canadian portraiture, as well as landscape. During the late eighteenth and early nineteenth centuries, anonymous itinerant portraitists painted with an objectivity and hard-edged style which was shared by realists more than a century later. Portrait painters who followed these early pioneers failed to sustain their frankness of statement, and the majority of late nineteenth-century painters of people dipped their brush in the soft, easy lines of flattery, muting the contours of face and figure to accommodate the sitters who commissioned them.

Two notable exceptions to this were Antoine Plamondon (1802-95) and his student, Theophile Hamel (1817-70). It is true that Plamondon, in particular, was not above producing commonplace portraits, conveying little character in either the features of the subject or the style of the painting. On many occasions, however, he executed studies which reveal a penetrating insight joined to a lean economy of technique. The relentless honesty of the pair of portraits of Thomas Paud and Mrs. Paud (1831 – Montreal Museum of Fine Arts), with their almost cutting sharpness of realism, prove how uncompromising a recorder Plamondon could be in the vigour of his twenties. Here there is none of the salon posturing evident in many of his later portraits.

Oddly enough, it is when he steps outside the field of portraiture that Plamondon reaches dramatically across more than a century to the high realists of today. His three versions of *Still Life with Apples and Grapes* (1870), and the mystical *The Flute Player* (1866), with their luminous colour and sharp dramatic backlighting, closely relate to modern realism in concept and feeling.

Theophile Hamel was a more incisive portrait painter than his teacher Plamondon. From the very beginning of his career, Hamel revealed a confident directness in his portraits, and a lean, basically linear style. A candid simplicity underlies the realism of such compelling portrayals as *Louis Joseph Papineau, Lord Durham with Three Indian Chiefs, Four Children and a Dog* (Musée du Québec) and *A Lady of the Molson Family and her Children* (Vancouver Art Gallery). As an aid to realism, both Hamel and Plamondon used photographs or daguerreotypes, from time to time, to assist them in their commissions.

The Royal Academy of Great Britain played a major role in the training of most of Canada's realistic painters in the nineteenth century.

Britain's official schools of art during the middle of the nineteenth century were dominated by strong-minded instructors dedicated to the discipline and craftsmanship demanded for achievements in the field of detailed realism. These professors were outstanding artists in their own right and could inspire by example as well as instruction. Many of Canada's prominent painters of the Victorian era benefitted directly from the experience of such luminaries of the period as Frederick, Lord Leighton (1830-96) and Sir John Millais (1829-96), both of whom served as Royal Academy Presidents, as well as Richard Redgrave, R.A. (1804-88) and J.R.Herbert, (1810-90). It was the high level of draughtsmanship and realism taught by such masters that emigrant-artists William Cruikshank, John Arthur Fraser, F.M.Bell-Smith and Charlotte Schreiber brought with them to Canada between the 1850's and 1870's. Their standards of craftsmanship had an important influence on the Canadian scene and a lasting effect on later generations of Canadian art students.

William Cruikshank (1849-1922) and John Arthur Fraser (1838-98) studied at London's Royal Academy School, while F.M.Bell-Smith (1846-1923) and Robert Harris (1849-1919) attended, respectively, the South Kensington School of Art and the Slade School, where the majority of instructors were full or associate Royal Academy members. Charlotte Schreiber (1834-1922) exhibited regularly with the Royal Academy before coming to Canada.

William Cruikshank was one of the most influential Canadian realists of his era. He taught in Toronto art schools for more than a quarter of a century, employing methods of instruction which were based on those of his own teachers, Leighton and Millais, at the British Royal Academy School. His teaching stressed drawing from the antique cast and on-the-spot pen-and-ink sketching – joyless but effective disciplines for anyone contemplating the making of accurate pictorial reports.

Cruikshank, a single, solitary and sarcastic presence in the Canadian art world, was born in Scotland, but lived most of his adult life in Toronto. He was almost fanatically devoted to the art of drawing, and filled countless sketch books at home and on his favourite travels along the shores of the St. Lawrence. He was an extremely gifted painter, and before he came to Canada had exhibited with the British Royal Academy between 1865 and 1879. He could easily have been the foremost Canadian realist of his time, but unfortunately he dedicated most of his energy to teaching pen-and-ink illustration rather than to his own painting. The quality of such works as *Anne Cruikshank* (Art Gallery of Ontario) and *Breaking a Road* (National Gallery of Canada) suggest how much Canadian art lost as a result.

CHARLOTTE SCHREIBER *Sleighing on the Credit*
Oil on canvas c.1875 32 x 43
Collection: Mr and Mrs Fred Schaeffer

WILLIAM CRUIKSHANK *Anne Cruikshank*
Oil on canvas c.1890 38-1/2 x 35-1/4
Art Gallery of Ontario

GEORGE A. REID *Forbidden Fruit*
Oil on canvas 1889 31 x 48
Art Gallery of Hamilton

Cruikshank did draw innumerable illustrations for the Canadian periodicals, however. It was an activity where his speed and precision as a draughtsman were displayed at their best. *Canadian Illustrated* and other journals which covered a wide range of sports and news owed much to his flair for this type of work.

In June of 1909 Cruikshank decided to present a large collection of his sketchbooks to the Art Gallery of Toronto. With them he sent a letter which revealed his characteristically forthright approach: "They [the sketch books] generally contain too much incident, and I was probably more concerned in getting character than observing the limitations of the pen, but they may be interesting from their intense individuality. . . . Cleverer and more complete drawings are done now from deliberately posed models at artists' clubs all over the world, with the ulterior possibility of photographic reproduction. But forty years ago, when photography was more restricted and there was no dry-plate process, the sketch book was the only means of collecting data of a necessarily more or less off-hand character."

A close colleague and friend of Cruikshank's who did not hesitate to utilize photography – and in fact began work in Canada as a photographer – was Frederick Marlett Bell-Smith. Bell-Smith, the son of the English painter, John Bell-Smith, emigrated to Montreal with his father at the age of twenty-one, after a period of training at the South Kensington School of Art in London, where he was born. For a short time after his arrival in Canada, he worked for William Notman, the Montreal photographer, and drew brilliant miniature watercolours of local events on Notman's tiny calling cards.

Schooled under the rigours of academic realism, Bell-Smith, like Cruikshank, possessed a ready facility as a draughtsman. He, too, applied this skill to recording events for the country's leading picture paper, the *Canadian Illustrated*. His reliability as a realist recorder brought him many commissions, such as the painting of *The Queen's Tribute to Canada* (Queen Victoria placing a wreath on the coffin of Sir John Thompson), a work for which the Queen posed.

As an artist, Bell-Smith is still much underrated. Too much attention has been given to the rather vaporous watercolours he turned out toward the end of his long life, and too little to the concise, carefully composed realistic canvases and brilliant oil sketches of his first fifty or sixty years. The best of the sketches have a bright sparkle and colour. And the finest of his large realist paintings, such as *Return to School* (1884 – London Public Library and Art Museum), *Picking Strawberries* and *Lights of City Street* (1894) are important records of daily life in Victorian Canada.

The modesty and dedication of this country's pioneer realist-oriented painters is underlined by the fact that at the age of fifty, with a well-established reputation at home, Bell-Smith decided to spend a period attending classes at the Académie Colarossi in Paris.

John Arthur Fraser, like Bell-Smith, began his career in Canada after studying art in London, England, his native city. He arrived with his family at Stanstead, in the Eastern Townships of Quebec, when he was in his early twenties, having previously spent several years at the Royal Academy School under the noted realists, Richard Redgrave and William Topham (1808-77).

Fraser was to divide much of his career between photography and painting, one pursuit intimately influencing the other. He also was employed by William Notman in Montreal, and began by painting scenic backdrops for portraits, a chore he shared with a number of other noted artists of the period. He later graduated to painting the photographs themselves.

Fraser's subtle skill at turning a portrait photograph into a seeming work of art, and his natural bent for business, led Notman to hire him, in 1868, as a partner in a Toronto branch known as Notman-Fraser. This studio, located on King Street in the downtown area, became a place of employment and a meeting ground for many of Toronto's leading painters. And Fraser, with his fastidious academic training, was unquestionably an influence on the local scene.

Involved as he was in his photographic business, Fraser, like William Cruikshank, gave less time to painting than we, today, might wish. But during his fifteen years in Toronto, he did create a small group of haunting, realistic landscapes. Most of these are small canvases, which compellingly evoke a mood of nature through subtly related tones and closely massed natural details. One of the best of these is the sunset scene of Lake Scugog (National Gallery of Canada), painted in 1873. It clearly reflects, as does most of his work at the time, the feeling of a moment of time suspended – a familiar characteristic of the painting of his former Academy teacher, Richard Redgrave.

Fraser left Toronto for the United States in 1883 and spent most of the rest of his life there, except for a trip to the Rocky Mountains in 1886, when he returned to Canada to carry out a series of landscape commissions for the Canadian Pacific Railway. Those mountain paintings lack the intimacy and warmth of his earlier Ontario and Quebec landscapes, however. They possess an almost Courbet-like breadth of realism and no longer dwell affectionately upon individual detail.

The relationship of photography to creative painting in the work of Fraser and his contemporaries deserves attention in the light of the role it plays in realism today. People often say of the high realists, "Oh, but they must use photographs!" as though this were a dubious or novel approach to painting. Photography as an aid to art is hardly new. It has been utilized ever since the French painter-inventor Louis Daguerre made the photo process practicable in 1837. Delacroix, Degas, Cézanne, Toulouse-Lautrec, Paul Gauguin, Vincent Van Gogh and Thomas Eakins are only a few of the artists who regularly, or occasionally, used photography. Some of them, like Degas and Eakins, took their own pictures, while others employed professionals. In all cases, these creative artists used the camera as a tool to heighten or simplify their way to a more vivid creative statement. Only the most casual viewer could compare the intense formal design and sharpness of focus, subtleties of texture, and mutation of colour to be found in successful high realism with the limited pictorial character of a photograph.

In Canada, photographic studios played a vital part in nineteenth-century painting (as did commercial design houses in the later Group of Seven period). The studios offered congenial employment to many gifted painters when they were unable to survive through the sale of their pictures or teaching alone. William Notman's studio was particularly noted in this connection, no doubt because the photographer's own early ambition to be a painter made him well disposed to encourage the talents of the artists who emigrated to Canada from abroad. Not only did his studio serve as a gathering place for artists, but the Toronto studio hosted the maiden exhibition of the Ontario Society of Artists in 1873.

Notman was highly successful in his profession, which not only included the making of straight portrait photographs, but also montages of composite photos using hand-painted backgrounds. He also used skilfully painted backdrops of seasonal landscapes against which he posed his sitters. Such combinations of painting and photography required the hiring of a considerable number of artists, and many of the greatest names in Canadian art worked for Notman studios. Otto Jacobi, John A. Fraser, Henry Sandham, C.J. Way, Adolphe Vogt and John Hammond worked for the Montreal studio. In the Toronto Notman-Fraser branch, many future Academicians, including Horatio Walker, Frederick A. Verner, Robert F. Gagen, F. McGillivray Knowles and Homer Watson, were employed.

One regular visitor to the Notman studio was Robert Harris, the painter of *The Fathers of Confederation.* In painting his famous group study, Harris used many of Notman's portraits of the Founding Fathers, taken during the 1864 Quebec Conference.

24

Robert Harris' style was inconsistent throughout his lifetime, wavering between romantic studies that placated the sitter, and penetrating, analytical portraits. These latter works of stark realism are his best; he was most at home as a frank realist.

The questionnaires Harris sent out while working on *The Fathers of Confederation* gives ample proof of his insistence on accuracy. Sent to the Quebec Confederation Conference delegates or their survivors, the questionnaires asked, "Is the colour of the face evenly distributed? Is there much colour in the cheeks? nose? lips? chin? Is the forehead much lighter than the rest of the face? Are the hands large or small? . . ." In all, the artist sought information on thirty-three points.

Moncrief Williamson, in his biography of the artist, records Harris' own notes for the portrait of the Honourable George Brown, one of the delegates: "Personal details – Black Coat / Shade wan enough under lid. Colour a little / Height 5.10 / Eyes blue-green / Dark little pores (pupils) / Hair originally dark, but not black / Eyebrows nut brown / General complexion rather warm. Not too red – but warm / Colour in more, a little, lips. / A little colour shave marks / Little colour in corner of eye."

Throughout his life, Harris was plagued by eye trouble, but his determination would not allow him to take creative short-cuts. His mania for detail inevitably had its frustrations. Of an impoverished Toronto boy who was posing for him Harris wrote, "His clothes are the principal trouble; he had a very picturesque old torn linen coat. . . . Last Monday the little wretch had it washed which, of course, created fearful ravages in its constitution, besides spoiling the colour. However, we rolled it on the floor until it regained its tone."

Further evidence of his strong bent toward realism is found in a letter written from France in 1878: "I am just in raptures with some pictures I have seen by Millet, a French painter, dead a few years since. They are all subjects from French peasant life, every one a perfect poem." (Jean François Millet, along with Gustave Courbet and Honoré Daumier, was considered the leader of the realist movement on the Continent at the time.)

Born in the Vale of Conway, North Wales, Harris had emigrated to Charlottetown, P.E.I. in 1856, as a child of seven. From boyhood it was his ambition to be a painter, and he received encouragement from both his family and the community. While still in his teens, and without any art schooling, he was commissioned to do portraits of the members of the Island's Executive Council, although his full-time job at fifteen was that of a surveyor. Those early self-taught endeavours, plus the early training he received in Boston from 1873, probably explain an

PAUL PEEL *Covent Garden Market, London, Ontario*
Oil on canvas 1883 27-3/8 x 37
London Public Library and Art Museum

elemental vigour of style that continued to mark the best of Harris' work throughout his career. Although he later attended the Slade School in London (1876) under the highly polished Alphonse Legros, and studied in Paris under Leon Bonnat, there remains a strong American accent in such vigorous compositions as *The Local Stars* (Centennial Art Gallery, Charlottetown) which might easily have been painted by a student of Thomas Eakins or even Winslow Homer. One wonders what American paintings Harris might have seen as a young man in his twenties, studying anatomy and painting in Boston.

For a short period between 1879 and 1881, Harris lived in Toronto, teaching antique drawing at the Ontario School of Art (later the Ontario College of Art) and illustrating for the Toronto *Globe*. One of his fellow instructors at the school was Charlotte Schreiber, an English artist who had come to Canada with her husband in 1875.

Like Cruikshank and Bell-Smith, Mrs. Schreiber had been trained in the English mid-Victorian school of close realism, mainly under the academic painter, J.R.Herbert. As a young woman she had exhibited regularly with the Royal Academy between 1855 and 1874, under her maiden name of Charlotte Mount Brock Morrell. She was not as ambitious as some of her male colleagues, but in such paintings as *Sleighing, Springfield on the Credit, Portrait of Mrs. Martin Grahame,* and *View of University College from Taddle Creek* she realized canvases with subtle personal style which are much more than mere period pieces.

Charlotte Schreiber was diligent in her pursuit of realism. She used as models the people around her studio home at Springfield on the Credit (now Erindale, Ontario). These included the future artist-naturalist, Ernest Thompson Seton (1860-1946), who was for years her student and protégé. To guarantee accuracy in her nature compositions, she kept a menagerie of squirrels, rabbits and other animals in her home. She was a keen photographer, and often used the camera as an aid to her creative work.

In an interview given to the Saturday *Globe* on March 2, 1895, she declared her realist bias: "The human hand, the fingernail, the foot, every portion of the human body, the parts of a flower are divinely beautiful. It is a joy to paint them as they are in reality. Is it not better to do so than to use that method which gives any structure when viewed near at hand the appearance of an indistinguishable blotch?"

In a review of her art in the same paper, a commentator noted, "One can look into the work and examine it minutely, even to the veining of the girl's feet, which are swollen from standing. She [the artist] adheres faithfully to detail, always subordinating the part, however, in a careful consideration of the whole."

ANTOINE PLAMONDON *Still Life with Apples and Grapes*
Oil on canvas c.1870 27-1/2 x 30-1/4
National Gallery of Canada

JULIAN R. SEAVEY *Music*
Oil on canvas 1890 36 x 22
National Gallery of Canada

After the death of her husband, Charlotte Schreiber returned to England in 1899, after twenty-four years in Canada. She died at Paignton, Devon, at the age of eighty-eight.

One of the students at the Ontario School of Art on King Street during the time that Robert Harris and Charlotte Schreiber taught there was George Reid (1860-1947), who was to become one of the most significant of all Canadian realists.

Reid was born at Wingham, Ontario, in the rural farmlands of Huron County. As a boy, he spent all of the time he could snatch from school and barnyard chores drawing copies of engravings from English illustrated papers. He enjoyed draughtsmanship, despite the discipline it required, thus displaying a natural bent toward the school of realism he would later follow.

Like most struggling farmers of the period, Reid's father looked upon the pursuit of art as an activity for the upper classes or, at best, a pastime. He did not object to George drawing as a hobby, but as he was in no position to support his son, frowned on it as a future profession.

When Reid did leave for Toronto in the autumn of 1878, he tried to get work in the photographic studios that specialized in hand-touched portraits. But his attempts were unsuccessful, and he was obliged to support himself as a machinist in the Toronto Foundry, working by day and attending art classes at the Ontario School by night.

Reid's natural talents and determination attracted the special attention of Robert Harris and Charlotte Schreiber. The esteem was mutual; years later, Reid remembered Harris, in particular, as a distinguished and inspiring teacher. Harris had a forthright approach to his subject matter, a directness of style, and a sense of Canadianism which appealed to the young student. The sympathy and rapport between teacher and student was affirmed when Reid painted a vigorous and faithful copy of the Harris canvas *News-boy* in 1880, during his last term at the Ontario School of Art.

At the end of that school year, Reid returned to Wingham to try his luck in the market place, and his rural portrait studio turned out to be surprisingly successful. Within a few months, his commissions to portray local residents brought him a steady income. He charged $25 for a head-and-shoulders and $40 for a three-quarter-length portrait. Within a year he had saved enough to realize his ambition to study with the great American realist master, Thomas Eakins, about whom he had read in an art magazine. Equally important, the Pennsylvania Academy of Fine Arts in Philadelphia, where Eakins taught, offered Painting from the Figure, something not yet taught at the modest Ontario School of Art.

Reid arrived in Philadelphia in October 1882. Under Eakins, he began the severe training required of any true realist of the period. As well as painting from the nude model, he studied perspective, visited operating theatres and dissected corpses for anatomy, did field photography, and studied the figure out of doors.

Sculpture was an important part of the training Eakins offered. He believed that sculpting provided a more complete understanding of the forms his students would eventually be painting, and he modelled figures in the round for his own compositions, prior to painting them. George Reid adopted this approach and continued to use it throughout his long career.

Eakins consciously based his art on science. He recommended higher mathematics to his students because it was "so like painting." He remarked about his deep commitment to dissection: "One dissects simply to increase his knowledge of how beautiful objects are put together, to the end that he may be able to imitate them. Even to refine upon natural beauty – to idealize – one must understand what he is idealizing." Fairfield Porter, in his book on Eakins, recorded how deliberately the artist prepared his subjects: "He posed the model in exactly the same position every day, relative to a grid placed vertically behind her, with a place on the wall in front of her to look at. He attached coloured ribbons to salient points of the dress corresponding to points on the grid. The canvas was perpendicular to the floor and at right angles to the eye of the painter. The painting thus became a projection of the figure on a vertical plane, like an architectural elevation."

In his famous painting *Max Schmitt in a Single Scull,* Eakins laid out the entire scene by mathematical calculations. All forms and shadows were plotted mechanically. The positions of the waves and boats were traced on the final canvas from mechanical drawings done on tracing paper. Many of today's high realists use a similar method.

By the time he had completed his three years at the Pennsylvania Academy under Eakins, George Reid had a knowledge of his craft that has rarely been equalled by any other Canadian. He later passed on Eakins' approach to realism to his own students – men such as C.W. Jefferys and Frederick Challener, who were to make secure reputations of their own.

Part of a letter written by Reid while studying at Philadelphia could almost have been expressed by one of today's realists: "Eakins teaches the highest sort of realism, and that is the direction I wish to go. His figures are rendered as though sculpted and fixed for all time in their own immediate surround." Reid made trips to England in 1885 and to France in 1888, but his guiding spirit in art remained Thomas Eakins.

When he finally resettled in Toronto in 1889, Reid created a series of reflections of his rural Ontario boyhood which, by themselves, are sufficient to earn him a leading position in any history of Canadian realism.

Reid's Toronto studio was a large loft above the Arcade Building on Yonge Street in the city's downtown area. There he painted such familiar Canadian masterpieces as *The Story* (Winnipeg Art Gallery) and *Forbidden Fruit* (1889 – Art Gallery of Hamilton). Although these paintings of rural boyhood are very different in composition (*The Story* has five figures, while *Forbidden Fruit* is a solo study), Reid utilized the same setting for both. To guarantee realism *à la* Eakins, he turned one-half of his 18′ x 20′ studio into a replica of a hayloft. He constructed a scaffolding of logs and imported dozens of bales of hay to spread across it. For models, he hired local boys from the studio's downtown neighbourhood. (Reid later recalled that he had read *Tales of the Arabian Nights* in a hayloft like the one recorded in *Forbidden Fruit*.) It was fitting that this early masterpiece was exhibited in 1891 in the Philadelphia Academy where he learned the skills displayed in it.

Much of Reid's later work fails to retain the intensity of realism displayed in his early works – *Forbidden Fruit, The Story, Going to Church, Shingle Making, Carrying Hod* and *The Apple-paring Bee* and others – but he continued to insist, even in 1947, at eighty-six, that "the function of art is to represent life."

A fellow-Canadian who had preceded George Reid in studying at the Pennsylvania Academy was Paul Peel (1860-91), the son of a London, Ontario drawing teacher and marble cutter. Peel worked under Thomas Eakins from 1877-1880, but his talents were not to be bent as far toward realism as Reid's. The maturity of his tragically brief career was to be devoted mainly to a softly rendered, often romantic view of life.

But the frank realism of Eakins' teaching did prevail in a number of canvases painted by Peel immediately after his return to Canada from Philadelphia. A typical example of this brief period of crisp, brilliantly lit realism is the 1883 street scene, *Covent Garden Market, London, Ontario*. In this painting, every shadow, each cloud, bird, building, horse and figure are fixed relentlessly in space. It is a wonderfully candid composition, the product of a typical New World vision.

Another artist who, like Peel, limited his excursions into close realism to the early part of his career, was Homer Watson (1855-1936).

Born in Doon, Ontario, Watson was one of the many artists who worked at Toronto's Notman-Fraser photo studio during his early years. As a nineteen-year-old, self-taught novice, Watson probably benefitted from his association with such senior artists as Lucius O'Brien, the founding President of the Royal Canadian Academy, who like Watson, was self-taught.

The deepest impact upon Watson's early career came from his trip in 1876 to New York State, where he came to know the Adirondack Mountains and the Hudson River Valley and saw for the first time the paintings of the Hudson River School artists. These works, particularly those of Thomas Cole, made a deep impression on him. The romantic high realism of Cole manifested itself sharply in Watson's art for the next decade. The eerily lit *Death of Elaine* (1877 – Art Gallery of Ontario), *Landscape with River* (1878 – Art Gallery of Ontario), *A Coming Storm in the Adirondacks* (1879 – Montreal Museum of Fine Arts), *On the Grand River at Doon* (1880 – National Gallery of Canada), *On the Old Stage Road, November Night* (1881 – Art Gallery of Hamilton) – all show that combination of precise observation and romantic mood which reflects the pervading impact made upon him during his twenties by Thomas Cole.

During his thirties, Watson came under the more mellow influence of the canvases of George Inness, an American artist he had met in 1876, but who did not shape his work until a decade later.

For many years, Watson's later, broadly executed compositions commanded the most attention and the deepest appreciation. Today, the more severe early paintings are supplanting those later canvases in the affection of many observers looking for a more precise and less generalized creative approach.

High realism in still-life painting began in the New World with the American painter Raphaelle Peale (1774-1825), who created his incredibly convincing facsimile of tickets, invitations and newspapers called *A Deception* in 1802.

Peale was followed by a succession of brilliant American *trompe l'oeil* artists throughout the nineteenth century, terminating in the two masters of this style, William Harnett (c. 1851-95) and John Frederick Peto (1854-1907). Strangely, Canada produced little in this field of high realism which, at the time, was being received with vast popularity by the public and collectors.

An exceptional high realist was Julian Ruggles Seavey (1857-1940), who painted, in 1890, a remarkable still life of a violin and sheet music, entitled *Music* (National Gallery of Canada). The work is strongly reminiscent of Harnett's. A second work, in the Art Gallery of Hamilton,

WILLIAM G.R. HIND *View from Sunnyside*
Oil on panel c.1880   12-1/2x9-1/4
Private Collection

Wild Raspberries, is closer to such American mid-Victorian realists as William Mason Brown (1828-98) and John William Hill (1812-79).

Julian Seavey was American by birth, from Boston, and was educated in New York and Europe before moving to Hamilton, Ontario, in 1879. From 1884 to 1895 he taught in London, Ontario, and in St. Thomas at Alma College. Returning to Hamilton, he taught at Hellmuth Ladies College for thirteen years and finally at the Hamilton Normal School until his retirement in 1931. As an artist, Seavey was clearly a victim of the economic necessity to teach. The two still lifes for which he is now best known suggest the kind of work he might have done had he not been forced to instruct young ladies and prospective teachers.

A much more subtle and individual painter of still life was Seavey's Quebec contemporary, Ozias Leduc (1864-1955). His small *Still Life* of 1892 challenges the best *trompe l'oeil* painters of the United States. Its delicacy of tone and draughtsmanship are the more remarkable for being achieved by a self-taught craftsman.

Leduc was born in the village of Saint-Hilaire, near Montreal. Early in life he showed the quiet determination which made him one of the purest of all Canadian painters. His small easel paintings were executed between long periods of church decoration, his chief profession.

It is Leduc's paintings of the 1880's which most closely relate to high realism. The brightly lit, almost flat design of his *Boy with Bread* (c. 1882-84 – National Gallery of Canada) is remarkably modern in the simplicity and economy of its presentation. The haunting candlelit still life of 1893, *The Farmer's Supper* (National Gallery of Canada) shows another aspect of Leduc's vision, no less exact in the way it is observed, but capturing the quiet domestic drama found in such masters as Jean-Baptiste Chardin or the brothers LeNain.

Leduc made one trip to Europe, in 1897, but although it introduced some suggestion of impressionist broken colour into his work, his outlook and style remained basically the same throughout his career. In his *Portrait of Mrs. Bindorf,* done in the 1930's, we find the same unaffected vision and the painstaking manner of applying paint that marked his canvases of the 1880's.

The major influence on high realism in Canada during the first half of the twentieth century came from the American Precisionist movement. The Precisionists were a group of artists, mostly based in New York, who through severe discipline, logic and consummate technique, stripped their subjects, whether bars, industrial plants, still lifes or machines, to their essential visual facts. The best Precisionist paintings possess an almost hallucinatory lucidity and are markedly North American in character.

OZIAS LEDUC *Boy with Bread*
Oil on canvas 1892-99 20 x 22
National Gallery of Canada

The Precisionist movement had its beginnings during the 1920's and its influence has continued into the seventies. Its members were dedicated to an intensely high realism, in which the technical means of creating the picture were restrained so that the object portrayed had the maximum impact *as an object*. The Precisionists disdained the parading of expressionist impasto brush strokes, so beloved of the abstract action painter. Their surfaces are smooth and deliberately impersonal. The creative impact comes from the design, editing, and flawless definition of their pictorial material.

The Precisionists were artists who shared a similar outlook on painting, but were not organized into a fixed exhibiting group. Among them were some of the most celebrated of American painters: Georgia O'Keefe (1887-   ), Charles Demuth (1883-1935), Niles Spencer (1893-1952), Joseph Stella (1877-1946), Preston Dickinson (1891-1930) and Charles Sheeler (1883-1965).

Charles Sheeler was the unquestioned master of the Precisionists, and its main spokesman. In a catalogue for his one-man exhibition at New York's Museum of Modern Art in 1939, Sheeler spoke for most high realists when he wrote, "In art school the degree of success in the employment of the slashing brush was thought to be evidence of the success of the picture. Today it seems to me desirable to remove the method of painting as far as possible from being an obstacle in the way of consideration of the content of the picture."

Andrew Wyeth made a similar statement in his notes for the Museum of Modern Art's group realist show of 1943: "My aim is to escape from the medium with which I work. To leave no residue of technical mannerisms to stand between my expression and the observer. To seek freedom through significant form and design rather than brush handling. Not to exhibit craft, but rather to submerge it, and make it rightfully the handmaiden of beauty, power and emotional content."

Sheeler helped form the creative attitudes and styles of two leading Canadian painters during the thirties and forties – LeMoine FitzGerald (1890-1956) and Bertram Brooker (1888-1955). Sheeler's philosophy and that of his fellow Precisionists also touched the work of Charles Comfort (1900-   ), particularly in his choice of subject matter.

These three Canadian artists shared friendship as well as painting styles. Brooker and Comfort often came together in Toronto during the 1930's, as FitzGerald and Brooker did during the latter's trips to Winnipeg. The letters between FitzGerald and Brooker refer, from time to time, to members of the American Precisionist group. In a letter written in the summer of 1933 Brooker relates, "Charles [Comfort]

L. LEMOINE FITZGERALD *From an Upstairs Window, Winter*
Oil on canvas 1948 24 x 18
National Gallery of Canada

liked my stuff very well. He thought the one done on the top deck of the boat on the way home was a little like a Sheeler and felt the same thing about one of a waterfront scene made a couple of nights before we left Toronto."

Both Brooker and FitzGerald were ready with praise of Sheeler and the other Precisionists, and acknowledged a relationship to them in their work of the 1930's and 1940's. American critics also noted a kinship, and in a review of the first Canadian Group Exhibition, held in Atlantic City in 1933, one writer referred to FitzGerald's *Dead Tree* as having "a delicacy reminiscent of Georgia O'Keefe."

LeMoine FitzGerald was born in Winnipeg and, except for brief trips, spent his entire life there. He had a deep affection for the familiar forms which he came to know more intimately with the passing years. Most of his masterpieces portraying simple Winnipeg area scenes are presented with an astonishing personal sensibility of tone and touch, but are straightforward and undistorted in their factual point of view. This is especially true of such canvases of the 1930's and 1940's as *From an Upstairs Window* (1948 – National Gallery of Canada), *Dr. Snider's House* (1931 – National Gallery of Canada), *Jar* (1938 – Winnipeg Art Gallery) and such chalk drawings as *Jug on a Window Sill* (c. 1943) and *Chris' Barn* (c. 1949).

FitzGerald stated his basically realist philosophy and the discipline demanded by it when he wrote, "One who thinks of the artist in this [an idealistic] way has never sat in the open prairie on a none too comfortable stool, the thermometer registering maybe 100 degrees, and tried for six to eight hours at a stretch to capture on paper or canvas some organized semblance of the ever-changing cloud forms of the sky. Nor has he stood for hours struggling with the wind-blown forms of trees or, again, in the late fall, when the frost is in the air, put down with numbed fingers the delicate harmony of naked trees against the sky."

Bertram Brooker, though a pioneer Canadian abstractionist, gave much of his career to painting works of high realism. Brooker found a special pleasure and creative satisfaction in doing immaculately rendered still lifes of commonplace things like vegetables, ski boots and baskets. Such canvases as *Still Life with Bag No. 3*, or *Still Life with Apples and Pepper* are models of subtly modelled, smooth-surfaced realism. They are cool in character and pristine. Some of Brooker's drawings of landscapes are superb examples of graphic high realism. Executed with pencil, they were patiently drawn on the spot, sometimes requiring a full day for their completion.

During the 1930's, Charles Comfort painted the industrial and rural architectural themes explored so effectively by Charles Sheeler in the

United States. No humanity is evident to disturb the autonomy and drama of the structures themselves. Like the American Precisionists, Comfort reduced the paint texture in his works to an almost smooth surface, with only a suggestion of impasto. He also utilized a very limited palette of colours, to stress the dramatic backlighting which is usually featured in his portrayals of architecture.

The best of these Comfort canvases of the 1930's included *Lake Superior Village* (1937 – Art Gallery of Ontario), *Tadoussac* (1938 – National Gallery of Canada) and a few penetrating portraits, such as the *Self-portrait in August* (1934).

D. P. Brown

A number of Canada's best contemporary high realists were associated in their formative years with veteran realist Alex Colville during his period as an art teacher at Mount Allison University, in Sackville, New Brunswick. Among the foremost of these is Dan Price Brown, whose small, fastidiously wrought egg-tempera paintings have won him a following among prominent collectors in Canada and the United States. That following is inevitably restricted, since Brown's annual production is limited to three or four paintings and a few drawings in pencil, pen or silverpoint.

Brown is a classic example of today's high realist in his devotion to the discipline, industry and craftsmanship required of anyone working in this demanding creative area. For the realist, the first flame of inspiration must be sustained through exacting processes which require the maximum of technical skill. There are no shortcuts in this field.

Brown's own career has been devoid of shortcuts. His life has been divided between Europe and Canada, and he has become acquainted with the best art of both. He has taken full advantage of his opportunities, has assiduously studied the paintings of the great masters, and has worked painstakingly to perfect his own craft.

Born in Forestville, Ontario in 1939, Dan and his twin sister, Abigail, were adopted at the age of six months by Mr. and Mrs. John Price Erichsen-Brown of the community of King, just north of Toronto. Their home overlooked a ravine through which a stream ran, and in which raspberry canes, mint, frogs and chipmunks flourished – subject matter Brown was later to incorporate into his art.

Dan first came into serious contact with art through his grandfather, a prominent lawyer and amateur painter, Frank Erichsen-Brown, at whose summer place in Go-Home Bay, Ontario, he met such noted artists as A. Y. Jackson, F. H. Varley and Will Ogilvie. The Erichsen-Brown cottage was located in the heart of Georgian Bay's "Group of Seven country," and from the age of twelve Dan had the privilege of going out on sketching trips with Jackson and Ogilvie, both of whom would stay for prolonged periods on the family island. He watched them paint and listened to critical bull sessions as they discussed one another's work. Furthermore, virtually every member of the Erichsen-Brown family painted or drew to some extent, and art was a common topic of conversation.

Since his father belonged to the consular service, Dan moved about more in his formative years than most children do. But wherever the family was posted, his mother continued to encourage his early predilection for art. His father served in Brussels for several years, and during that time, when he was in his middle teens, Dan attended the

The Young Canadian
Egg tempera on panel 1968 11 x 16
Collection: Dr N.M. Jolly

The Wedding Tray
Egg tempera on panel 1968 24 x 30
Collection: Senator John Aird

The Hawk
Egg tempera on panel 1971 16x38
Collection: Senator John Aird

Detail of *The Hawk*

Eerde School, a Quaker boarding establishment near Ommen in Holland. In the seventeenth-century moated manor house and stables which housed the Eerde students, Brown met instructors who gave him an intensive introduction to the history of art. His own favourite paintings were the works of the High Renaissance, and he was encouraged to copy them in pencil and chalk.

The most rewarding portions of those European years, however, were the summer trips he took with his mother, sister and brother, Adam, to the great art centres of Florence, Rome, Venice, Assisi, Amsterdam, Bruges, Paris and Ghent. In those places he encountered the art of Leonardo da Vinci, Titian, Vermeer, Rogier Van der Weyden, Jan van Eyck and Pieter Bruegel. To this day these works represent for him the ideal in conception and technique.

At seventeen, Dan was sent to England to attend the private school of Clayesmore at Iwerneminster in Dorset, and his two years there confirmed his decision to be an artist. At the time, Lawren P. Harris was in London, England, on a sabbatical leave from directing Mount Allison's school of art. Brown had an opportunity to show Harris his drawings and paintings and was encouraged to go to the Sackville school. He enrolled at Mount Allison in mid-term of 1958.

During that period, the University's Fine Art Department was designed on the English system of gradual advancement. The first year was devoted almost exclusively to drawing. Throughout the course there were the constant disciplines of drawing from the antique cast, perspective, anatomy and life classes – the very basis necessary to any painter with ambitions in the field of high realism. Brown's instructors at Mount Allison included Lawren P. Harris and Alex Colville, as well as Edward B. Pulford, a teacher whose basic training he remembers with appreciation. At that time Alex Colville taught anatomy, mural painting, sculpture and the history of art. Most important, he brought his own paintings to class and analyzed them for the students. Those paintings and the introduction to the egg-tempera medium had a powerful formative influence on Brown.

Another future high realist, Christopher Pratt, was attending Mount Allison at that time. Both Brown and Pratt insisted on living off campus, and did much of their experimental painting independently, away from the direct supervision of the university. Both had difficulty, from time to time, in adjusting to a set teaching schedule – thus displaying a spirit of individuality that may have been partly responsible for their later success in developing markedly personal styles. Today Brown insists that the work he did independently during his years at Mount Allison was as vital to his career as the direct tuition in class.

Three Leaves
Egg tempera on panel 1971 11-1/4 x 13
Collection: Mr Jules Stoormer

At the Piano
Egg tempera on panel 1972 15 x 13
Collection: Senator John Aird

At the end of three and a half years at Mount Allison, Brown went to the family farm in Aurora, Ontario, and lived there alone for several years while his father was serving as the Canadian Consul in New York City. On the farm he began to put together all that he had learned in Europe and in the university, and to apply it to his familiar native Ontario landscape. He enthusiastically drew the rural countryside around the family farm, using pen-and-ink, or silverpoint – an ancient technique he had first learned in Holland. (Silverpoint technique involves drawing upon a specially prepared paper with a silverpointed stylus, instead of lead pencil. It lends itself to very delicate and detailed renderings and is a favourite tool of many modern high realists.)

Dan Brown's first major painting – of a young girl in autumn, with her hair blown by the wind – was completed at Aurora in 1962. It was bought for $200 by Douglas Duncan, who ran Toronto's Picture Loan Society and who, during his lifetime, was patron and friend to many of Canada's leading artists. That first sale at twenty-two was important to Brown, who was beginning to have doubts about his choice of lifework, so different from his father's.

It was his father's position as Canadian Consul in New York City that first brought Brown's work to the attention of a major dealer. During February of 1963 Alex Colville held an exhibition at Manhattan's Banfer Gallery, and a reception was given in the artist's honour by John Price Erichsen-Brown. Dan attended the reception, taking with him some recent paintings to show his former teacher. Alex Colville recommended him to the Banfer Gallery owners, and Brown joined Colville as one of their exhibitors. This was an important event to the young artist, who had offered his works to Toronto commercial dealers and had been turned down.

Brown continued to exhibit with the Banfer Gallery until late 1968. The first painting he showed with them in New York was *Julia* (1963), a portrait of his niece against a weather-beaten door at the Brown farm. From then on, he exhibited at Banfer such major egg temperas as *Fallen Time* (1963), *Put to Pasture* (1964), *Abandoned* (1963), *Indian Summer* (1966), *Soon* (1966), *The Wedding Tray* (1967-68) and *Cat at Window* (1968).

In the Banfer years, Brown's paintings were inevitably dominated by his farm environment. With the major exceptions of *Beatrice* (1967) – a variation on a portrait by Leonardo da Vinci of Beatrice d'Este – and *The Wedding Tray* (a double portrait of himself and his wife), most of the 1963-69 works comprise a tribute to his Aurora experience. *Kettleby Creek,* of 1968, goes even further back, to recreate the stream he played along during his early childhood at his parents' farm in King.

Despite their basic unity of rural subject matter, the paintings of 1963-69 exhibit important technical changes and advances. The increased enrichment and authority in the artist's use of egg tempera, which lies between the portrait of his niece, *Julia,* of 1963, and a second portrait of the same sitter, *The Young Canadian,* of 1968, reveals Brown's capacity for evolving as an artist while working in a classic, technically demanding medium. *Julia,* for all its concision of drawing and attention to textures, reveals a dryness of brushwork and hesitancy in its approach to colour – qualities shared by *On the Fence* of the same year. These are tentative works, in which the artist's deliberate search for form is evident. By 1966, such panels as *Soon* and *Indian Summer* display an assurance with the egg-tempera medium which is superbly revealed in *The Young Canadian* of 1968 and *The Wedding Tray,* finished the same year.

The Wedding Tray was painted following his marriage, in 1966, to Mary Hierlihy of Edmunston, New Brunswick. It is the first of a series of portraits of his wife, who reappears later as the model for *The Reader* (1970) and *The Letter* (1971).

Coincidentally with Brown's coming of age as a high realist was his exhibition with Toronto's Dunkelman Gallery, early in 1969. Since then, the gallery has held two one-man shows of his work (in 1970 and 1972). Those two exhibitions clearly established him as one of the small group of important high realists working in Canada. *The Wedding Tray, At the Piano* (1972), *The Letter* and *The Hawk* (1971) are pictures both consummate in craftsmanship and original in vision. They pay ready tribute to the masters he admires (he includes a print of Vermeer's *View of Delft* hanging behind the figure of his wife in *The Letter*) but are true reflections of his own individuality.

At present Dan Brown lives in the Ontario town of Collingwood, with his wife and two daughters. His studio, in the attic of their red brick Victorian house, can only be reached by climbing up a fixed vertical ladder. It is a neat, almost bare room, with a northern exposure and is ornamented only by a few reproductions of works by his favourite artists.

Brown's technical approach to painting is as orderly as his studio. He paints only by day, since he feels he can control the tonal subtleties of his colours better by natural than by artificial light. He works in a small corner of the studio, where all of his equipment and materials are readily at hand. These include a clean sheet of glass, which serves as a mixing palette, a row of jars containing dry powdered pigments, nesting china saucers for holding wet paint, and a small container for egg yolk.

The Letter
Egg tempera on panel 1971 16 x 13-1/2
Collection: John Rykert

Woodcrust
Pen and coloured inks   1966   26 x 40
Private Collection

Indian Summer
Egg tempera on panel   1966   20x20
Collection: Henry Fonda

The pastes, composed of powdered pigments, water and egg yolk, are mixed together in the classic egg-tempera manner. As do most painters working in the centuries-old egg medium, Brown uses small red sable brushes to apply the resulting pigment to a hard, pristine-white gesso ground. He mixes the gesso from whiting and rabbits'-skin glue, and applies it to both sides of a one-quarter-inch K-3 pressed board. (He once used masonite, but finds its tendency to warp a handicap.) He insists on preparing his own gesso grounds, usually laying on five or six coats, smoothing each with sandpaper and emery-paper, and giving it a final wiping over with a damp cotton handkerchief. The resulting surface is as smooth as a marble table top.

Using tracing paper, Brown then transfers a detailed preparatory drawing on to the gessoed panel, reinforcing the basic outlines by incising them lightly with a silverpoint stylus. Once he begins the actual painting, he works from the background of his composition forward, starting with the sky in a landscape. He generally develops the forms by beginning with the light tones and working toward the darks, employing a wide range of colours on his palette – most of the permanent blues, reds, greens, yellows, black, white and earth colours.

With such simple resources, Dan Brown continues to add to that body of painstaking work which, though small in quantity, has enriched the totality of Canadian realism.

Jack Chambers

Anyone who accuses high realists of lazily accepting visual facts at surface value should study the art of Jack Chambers. As painter and theorist, he has relentlessly explored the nature of realism as a mirror of human existence. In his search, he has moved consciously through more realist variations than any other Canadian painter.

Apart from years of study in Europe, Chambers has lived in London, Ontario since his birth there in 1931. By the age of twelve, he was already developing his skills as an artist by copying postcards in oil colours. At fourteen, he had one of the few abstract paintings he has ever done accepted for the annual Western Ontario Art Exhibition at the London Public Library and Museum.

While he was at the H. B. Beal Technical School, Chambers studied art books in the local library, responding enthusiastically to the paintings of Masaccio, Giotto and the Byzantine period – all of which have remained touchstones throughout his career. During this formative period, he painted a number of portraits, including evocative studies of his grandfather, *John McIntyre* (1948) and his sister, *Shirley* (1948).

When he was eighteen Jack left technical school in mid-term, to spend the winter months travelling in Mexico. There he first saw the art of Jose Clemente Orozco who became, along with the English painter Stanley Spencer, one of his favourite twentieth-century artists. When he returned to London in the spring, he took the first of a long series of part-time jobs, and remained a Sunday painter for the next few years. A compelling *Self Portrait* (1952) of this period clearly reflects his attachment to Byzantine art, and also suggests some of the impact of Orozco.

By 1953 Chambers had saved enough money to realize his ambition to study in Europe. He sailed from New York in October on a Greek liner bound for Naples. For the next few months he travelled to Rome and Gratz, Austria, where he executed a number of superb drawings. In the Austrian town he wrote some poetry, and he says, "jogged along euphorically" in the shadow of such favourites as Van Gogh and Dylan Thomas. But even in that romantic mood, he found the winter in Gratz too cold, and headed by train for southern France, to get warm. There he met Picasso who suggested he might study in Barcelona. He left for Spain the same afternoon.

Still restless, Chambers soon left Barcelona and continued on to the island of Majorca. There he remained for several months in a fishing village on the northeast coast. In tiny Pollenca, a local shopkeeper and amateur painter gave Jack a pamphlet describing the Royal Academy School in Madrid. He also gave him an introduction to Jose Manaut Vigliette, a traditional painter in that city. In Madrid Vigliette took the

Madrid Window No. 2
Oil, pencil, paper and plexiglass 1968-69 45 x 40
Collection: Mr and Mrs Milton E. Harris

Unravished Bride
Oil on wood 1961 48 x 43
Collection: Mr and Mrs Geoffrey Rans

young Canadian under his wing, found him a pension in the city's workers' quarters, and got him enrolled as a casual student.

Chambers spent the spring of 1954 at the Academy, drawing plaster casts preparatory to taking his *ingresso,* an examination he was required to pass for entrance as a formal, full-time student. The Madrid Academy School is one of the most respected art academies in the world and possibly the most demanding. Jack failed his first entrance examination (a drawing done in two weeks) at Madrid in June, but after drawing all summer, succeeded in passing it in Valencia in September. In order to pay his school fees and support himself, he taught English three nights a week at a Madrid language school for the next two years, improving his own Spanish in the process.

Madrid's Academy is in an ancient building which houses its own magnificent collection of paintings by Velasquez, Goya, El Greco, Zurbaran and other Spanish masters. Chambers had the Academy collection and the incomparable Prado Museum readily available for the next five years. They provided an exposure to the actual styles, brushwork and scale of great works of art which no amount of reading or reproduction can approach. The illustrated books he had borrowed back in London, Ontario had not prepared him for the splendour of the originals.

The Royal Academy probably has the most rigorous schedule of any art school in the world. After completing its five-year course, there are few disciplines of visual art the graduate cannot undertake. Chambers did not always find it easy to survive during those years, but at the end of his second year, in 1956, his financial fortunes were improved when he received, from the Elizabeth R. Greenshields Foundation, a grant of $900. This was a large amount for a student who was able to buy a three-course meal for about 50 cents at the university restaurant. In 1958, at the end of his fourth year, Chambers won the Academy's Paular Scholarship in landscape painting, and the State Prize for figure painting.

Toward the end of his Academy training, Chambers became converted to Catholicism. "I became a Catholic," he says, "because I felt all of my energies needed discipline and control. I was very consciously looking for a spiritual container, and Catholicism supplied it." Chambers has remained a practising Catholic since, and many of the elements in his paintings refer to his concern for Christianity.

There is almost an icon quality in a large painting completed by Chambers during his last year at the Madrid Academy. *The Farewell* (1958-59) is an important transition work, containing the nucleus of many of his later works. It represents a dramatic pause in time, as a family of father, mother and three infants watch a train pulling away into the distance. The handkerchiefs held by the mother and the oldest child have a religious significance for Chambers. They are triangular shapes that represent the Christian dove of resurrection, as do the sailboat forms in *Regatta No. 1* (1968), where the portrait of a child who was drowned appears.

Resurrection, Chambers insists, has always been the dominant theme of his work. Such concepts as the graveyard scene, *Olga Visiting Graham* (1964 – Vancouver Art Gallery), is not a portrayal of sadness, but one of joyous resurrection. The misunderstanding of many commentators regarding his intent about his work in this regard upsets Chambers. Too often he has been accused of melancholy. His themes are *life* figures, he says; they convey the triumph of life over death, not the presence of death in life.

After graduating from the Madrid Academy, Chambers moved to the village of Chinchon, south of Madrid, in the fall of 1959. There he painted an extraordinary series of symbolic paintings, almost caricature-like in their stark light and shade, and macabre distortion. They are reminiscent of some of the Mexican masters he studied in 1949, although Chambers himself sees in them more of the influence of Picasso's *Guernica* and the work of Joan Miró. Certainly Miró's presence is evident in the powerfully composed *La Trilla* (1960), and some of Chamber's enthusiasm for Stanley Spencer may be seen in *Umbrella* (1959). *La Trilla* and *Umbrella,* the only subtle and serene canvases of the brief Chinchon period, are in strong contrast to such grotesque compositions as *Man and Dog* (1959), *Flying Saint* (1960) and *Man and Landscape* (1960). The strangely tubular creatures found in these visions are almost consciously primitive in their stress of each isolated form.

In April 1961, Chambers' mother took seriously ill, and he returned to London. Although he had at first planned to go back to Spain, he settled permanently in his home town. His Argentinian fiancée Olga Sanchez Bustos eventually joined him there, and they were married in August 1963.

The first works done in London were dramatically different from anything Chambers had done in Spain. Both style and theme had undergone a sudden and drastic change. Gone were the tormented forms of the Chinchon canvases; they were replaced by lyric linear arrangements of gold, pinks, quiet greens and greys representing subjects of almost dreamlike gentleness.

In these paintings details of intense realism appear for the first time. This, and a subtly granulated surface, add a sense of mystery and fan-

Umbrella
Oil on canvas   1959   19 x 17-1/2
Collection: Dr and Mrs R.G. Woodman

Diego Asleep No. 1
Oil on wood 1972 48 x 48
Toronto-Dominion Bank Collection

Olga Near Arva
Oil on wood   1963   33-1/4 x 55-3/4
Montreal Museum of Fine Arts

Detail of *Diego Asleep No. 1*

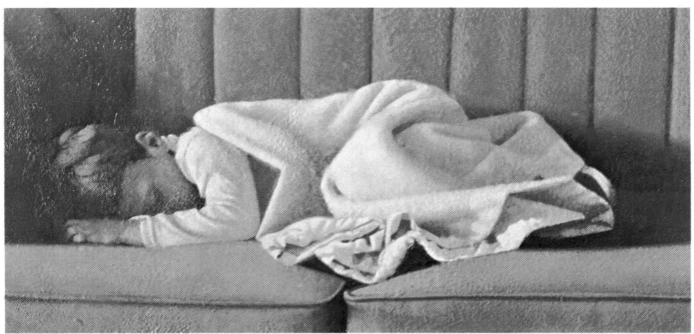

tasy to the paintings of the early 1960's, including the *Unravished Bride* (1961), *Five Shepherds* (1961-62), *Messengers Juggling Seed* (1962), *Olga at the South Pole* (1963) and *McGilvary County* (1962).

The paintings of 1961 through 1963 have a free-association of motifs, and Chambers refers to them as "composites" – juxtapositions of subjects brought together in a symbolic way. They represent his most specific "resurrection" compositions, freely bringing together dead and living people in a joyous sunlit setting. Sunshine and its yellow colour represent for Chambers their traditional symbolism of life, and many of his paintings of the early 1960's incorporate what he calls his yellow "spheres of energy" – symbols of spiritual existence.

Photography, which has played a large role in all of Chambers' art since he first used it as an aid in composing *The Farewell,* was involved from the very first in such London paintings as *Slaughter of the Lambs* (1961-62), and *Five Shepherds* which was based on snapshots made in an old people's home at Chinchon. The new texture and colour changes which occurred after his return from Spain he attributes to his new acquaintance with American abstract artists – Jackson Pollock, Hans Hofmann, Wilhelm de Kooning and others – whose work he had never seen in Europe.

After Chambers returned to London he not only made a drastic change in the style and concept of his work, but also began to use new materials. Quarter-inch plywood replaced canvas as a painting surface. This was covered with a dilute mixture of rabbit's-skin glue and marble dust, to give it a rough texture. The new working method is well represented by *Olga Near Arva* (1963 – Montreal Museum of Fine Arts), a composite of two photographs and one location. The children in the background are from an orphanage in Segovia where Chambers photographed them. The figure of Olga was photographed in a field near Madrid. The actual background was painted out of doors directly from nature at an intersection called Calamity Corners near London, Ontario.

In 1964 Chambers painted the first of a series of what he calls "fractured image" realist pictures. Among these were *Olga Visiting Mrs. V.* (1964), *Antonio and Miguel in the U.S.A.* (1965 – Art Gallery of Ontario), and *Olga and Mary Visiting* (1964-65 – London Public Library and Art Museum). In these, texture is reduced to a minimum and images are repeated in a montage way. In *Olga and Mary Visiting* Olga's head appears twice and Mary's hands holding a cup are repeated, with almost cinematic effect. The colour is muted in these paintings, reflecting Chambers' increasing desire to strip his forms down to their basics and emphasize form and shape until it is reduced, in *Olga, Diego and Gera-*

niums (1966), to almost a silver monochrome, with one isolated area of colour. Chambers was by then "saturated with colour," and as a change from it, he launched into a number of works executed solely in aluminum paint. "Silver gave me a rest from all the calculation required by colour. It also forced me to calculate formal values more intensely."

It was a logical step from these near-monochrome paintings to sculpture, and Chambers took that step in 1967 with a Canada Council grant. He went to Spain to study relief wood carving but was unsuccessful in finding the teacher he needed. As a substitute, he began a series of what he calls "relief drawings" in graphite with oil glazes on paper mounted on wood or plexiglass. These subtle and immaculate works are generally monochrome, multiple-image compositions, based on photographs and old still-life paintings. The best works in this genre include *Madrid Window No. 1* (1968), *Madrid Window No. 2* (1968-69), *Regatta No. 1* (1968), *Cat* (1967), and *The Hart of London* (1968 – National Gallery of Canada).

Chambers' interest in photography and painting merge completely in what he calls his "perceptual realism" pictures of 1968 to '73. Such paintings as *401 Towards London No. 1* (1968-69), *Diego Asleep No. 1* (1972), *Victoria Hospital* (1970), and *Mums* (1968-73) are virtually exact blow-ups of actual photographs. Chambers' contention is that the greatest sense of wonder can be found in the most familiar things, exactly transcribed. In an essay in the British magazine, *Arts and Artists* (Dec. 1972), Chambers discusses his creative philosophy of "perceptualism" at length. In it he remarks, "Perceptualism does not look back into the artist, but persists outwards beyond the object. . . . In the art of perceiving the world, man is linked intuitively with it. The more real the painting is, the more mysterious it is." He refers to the "peculiar impact of some paintings, where reality is so imminent that one feels he has stepped off the conveyor belt of time momentarily and actually glimpses the world in pause. Few paintings do this but when it happens the viewer on the outside looking in is able to experience the flow of time in which he is travelling and of which he is seldom, if ever, conscious."

Chambers' work has advanced by what he calls "leaps of style." The leaps began with *La Trilla* (1960), and occurred between *Five Shepherds* (1961-62), *Olga Visiting Mrs. V.* (1964), *Moving Side and Forward* (1967) and *401 Towards London No. 1* (1968-69). Each of these separate phases of Chambers' career has arisen from a passion to explore the nature of existence through the art of realism. Certainly no painter has given closer thought to his own concept of realism than he has, and few have brought to it more expert technical skill or a fresher inspiration.

Alex Colville

Alex Colville, the signal figure in Canadian high realism, has won international acclaim for his hypnotic and superbly crafted paintings. As a pioneer contemporary realist, he remained steadfast to his creative commitment during a prolonged period when official art circles were under the spell of abstraction. As an educator, he spent seventeen years helping to inspire future painters in the disciplines of their craft. Such leading realists as Christopher Pratt, D.P.Brown, Hugh Mackenzie and Tom Forrestall have benefitted by his example, and the determined progress of his career has inspired Canadian painters who have never had occasion to meet him.

Alexander Colville was born in 1920 in downtown Toronto, but spent his early childhood in the Niagara Peninsula city of St. Catharines, where his Scottish-born father was engaged as foreman of a steel gang. The Colville family moved to Amherst, Nova Scotia when Alex was nine, and since then he has lived always within a few miles of that Maritime community.

Unlike most artists, Alex Colville showed no serious interest in drawing until his late teens, when he met English-born painter Stanley Royle, who taught art at Mount Allison University in Sackville. Royle saw a few of Colville's haphazard efforts while he was inspecting the work of an art class held by a local lady painter. He was impressed, and recommended that Alex enroll in the Mount Allison art course. Colville today gives major credit for his career to the intense grounding in fine art fundamentals supplied by Royle, and it was in Royle's class that he met his future wife, Rhoda Wright of Kentville, Nova Scotia.

Colville graduated from Mount Allison with a Bachelor of Fine Arts degree in 1942, and immediately enlisted in the Canadian Army. He went overseas in May 1944. In November of that year he was appointed an Official War Artist, with the rank of captain – a post he kept until his discharge in June of 1946. During those two years, Colville depicted the progress of the war in the Mediterranean, Holland and Germany. His most successful and dramatic portrayals were recorded during the winter of 1944-45 with the Third Canadian Infantry Division in North-West Europe. There he sketched, in pencil, pen and watercolour, the casualties, corpses, prisoners and ruins which follow the advance of any army.

The war years were crucial to Colville's career as a painter. The harrowing scenes of desolation left a deep impact upon his approach to subject matter. He has often spoken of the presence of death in life and the importance of time in his pictures – ideas which were born, to a great extent, of his war experiences and observations. In a more im-

Hound in Field
Casein tempera on masonite   1958   30 x 40
National Gallery of Canada

Detail of *Hound in Field*

Woman Carrying Canoe
Acrylic on masonite 1972 19 x 33
Fischer Fine Art Limited, London

Study for *Woman Carrying Canoe*
Pen, wash and acrylic 1972 6-3/8 x 11
Collection: The Artist

mediate way, his service as a war artist offered him an ideal opportunity to draw and paint every day for two years, with almost complete freedom. Colville has said that the Canadian war art programme was a godsend to his progress as a painter. He was able to work close by older artists of great skill, and he particularly felt the influence and encouragement of Major Will Ogilvie, whose war art the younger painter deeply admired.

Altogether, Colville executed more than 125 works as a war artist. Most of these were on-the-spot watercolours and drawings, but fifteen were studio compositions in oil on canvas. The best of these larger paintings, such as *Exhausted Prisoners* of 1945, hint clearly at the considered, carefully edited compositions Colville was later to realize in his peacetime years. Here is the same meeting of men and machines, the same simplified sweeping contours and deliberate exploration of space. Even though done in oil, these war paintings have the lean, dappled build-up of form that one finds in his peacetime temperas.

After the war, Colville was torn between a career in commercial art and one as a teacher. Will Ogilvie persuaded him to accept a teaching position at Mount Allison University, and he remained there as an instructor from 1946 to 1963. This decision was made easier by what Colville describes as "a fantastic and deep emotional attachment to the Maritime Provinces," which had deepened during his war years abroad. He had married in 1942, and Sackville seemed to him the perfect domestic location to escape the overstimulation of the war.

Colville certainly didn't adopt a teaching career for the financial return; his annual income for the first year was barely $2,000. Nor did he find it a relaxed situation where he could find plenty of leisure time to paint. He painted only four oils and one watercolour during the first two years at Mount Allison, a dramatic change from his day-to-day production as a war artist. However, despite his work load as a teacher he managed to produce more than fifty paintings during the seventeen years he remained at Mount Allison – a measure of his determination.

Many of those paintings done between 1946 and 1963 were formative in both a technical and conceptual way. Almost doggedly, Colville seemed to be feeling his way, exploring many approaches to picture-making, and trying out a wide variety of technical media, searching for the one which would best assist him to express his creative urgings. During those seventeen years he shifted between straight oil, pure egg tempera, casein emulsion tempera, gum emulsion tempera (usually glazed with a mixture of stand oil and damar varnish), and oils with RES-N-GEL, a synthetic, jelly-like resin. The resulting paintings range from such tentative and almost coarsely rendered works as *Nude on a*

Rug (1954) and *Elm Tree at Horton Landing* (1956) to subtle and compelling technical performances such as *Boy, Dog and the Saint John River* (1958), *Hound in Field* (1958) and *Swimmer* (1962).

During his Mount Allison years, Colville seems to have been dominated by three basic themes: the nude female figure, animals and domestic life. After his experiences as a war artist, all three must have had a special, positive appeal for him. His first canvas after he was discharged from the army was *Three Horses* (1946 – Art Gallery of Ontario). This was followed by other equestrian studies, *Group of Horses* (1947), *Race Track, Sackville* (1950), *Two Pacers* (1951), *Girl on Piebald Horse* (1952), *Dog and Horse* (1953) and *Horse and Train* (1954 – Art Gallery of Hamilton). The first of the series of figure paintings was *Nude and Dummy* (1950 – New Brunswick Museum, Saint John). This was succeeded by *Nudes on Shore* (1950 – Beaverbrook Art Gallery, Fredericton), *Seated Woman* (1951), *Three Girls on Wharf* (1953), *Woman on Wharf* (1954) and *Nude on a Rug* (1954).

Between 1955 and 1960, Colville did a series of paintings which, perhaps unintentionally, celebrated domestic life around Sackville. These include *Family and Rainstorm* (1955 – National Gallery of Canada), *Woman at Clothesline* (1957 – National Gallery of Canada), *Child Skipping* (1958), *Boy, Dog and the Saint John River* (1958 – London Public Library and Art Museum), *Boy, Dog and School Bus* (1960) and *Mr. Wood in April* (1960). The fact that these paintings are universal in their creative power and human content, does not lessen the fact that they also remain, in a very real way, tributes to the specific domestic setting of their origin.

Colville had a real need for his teaching salary during his years at Mount Allison; his pictures found virtually no commercial market. From three one-man exhibitions (at the Hewitt Gallery, New York, in 1953 and 1955, and the Laing Gallery, Toronto, in 1958), he sold a total of four paintings. His determination and persistence with a demanding, time-consuming art in the face of such financial failure reflects his creative courage. His dedication finally paid off in February 1963, when his exhibition of twenty paintings at the Banfer Gallery in New York proved to be a sell-out. That success confirmed Colville's long-standing desire to leave teaching. It was followed in 1966 by international recognition when he was chosen Canada's representative at the famed Biennale Internazionale d'Arte in Venice. In 1965 he won the open competition to design Canada's Centennial coins. In 1969 he was given an exhibition at the Kestner-Gesellschaft in Hanover, Germany. In 1970 twenty-three of his paintings were shown in a major one-man exhibit at the Marlborough Fine Art Gallery in London,

January
Acrylic on masonite 1971 24 x 32
Toronto-Dominion Bank Collection

Woman at Clothesline
Oil emulsion on masonite   1957   48 x 36
National Gallery of Canada

England. And in 1971 he joined the Fischer Fine Art Gallery there as a regular exhibitor.

In 1963, at the time he left teaching to devote his full time to painting, Colville finally located a medium that met all of his creative requirements – acrylic polymer emulsion. Convenient, quick drying, mixable in water, and apparently permanent, acrylic colours (now universally popular) have remained his chosen medium. The restricted range of pigments available in acrylics is no limitation for Colville who uses only a small number of basic colours.

The acrylic paintings have caused unexpected and dramatic responses wherever they have been shown. European critics, in particular, have found in them "loneliness," "isolation" and "alienation." They find "devastation and the scent of death" in them. To this Colville says little. Typically, he remarked during a 1973 discussion about one of his small landscapes, *Snowstorm* (1971), "A painter is fundamentally a faker. If I say it is the sun in this painting, it is. If someone likes to see it as a moon, I have no quarrel." He has always insisted, "I paint almost always people and animals whom I consider to be wholly good, admirable and important." Certainly he constantly returns to favourite themes – his wife, animals, and the ever-present water which provides a firm horizon line for more than a quarter of his compositions.

Colville's working methods are governed by his slow, high-realist approach to art. He works in a small attic studio about twenty feet square on the third floor of his stucco home on Wolfville's main street. He normally paints for about four hours each morning, from 8:30 to 12:30, by the natural light of a west window, although he has no objection to artificial lighting. He does not use a mixing palette, but works directly from small china dishes, generally using a tiny sable brush. Unlike many realists, he keeps his picture panel almost vertical while he is painting on it.

Colville's acrylic polymer colours are limited to yellow ochre, burnt umber, burnt sienna, cadmium yellow light, cadmium red light, and cobalt blue, plus black and white. Until 1973 he used masonite panels as a painting surface, but then changed to K-3 board. He lays two coats of acrylic gesso to each side of the board. Although he usually makes about thirty preliminary drawings, Colville never prepares a full cartoon for a painting. He draws a geometric plan of his basic picture design in pencil, and then begins working directly with acrylics. On the average, it takes him four to six months to complete a painting.

Unlike many realists, Colville never uses the camera as an aid. During his years as a war artist, he constantly carried a camera to make detailed notes, but found that he could not use them when he came to compose

Church and Horse
Acrylic on masonite 1964 22 x 27
Montreal Museum of Fine Arts

Swimming Race
Glazed tempera on masonite   1958   24 x 38-1/2
National Gallery of Canada

a painting. On the other hand, he says that the motion picture may have affected his approach to art, particularly in relation to his sense of time.

The art of Alex Colville has survived some of the most pretentious verbiage and frantic footnoting ever visited upon a Canadian painter, but his own comments about art are fluent and unaffected. He shares with Jack Chambers the role of chief spokesman for Canadian realism. His comment, "I regard art not as a means of soliloquizing, but as a means of communication," could be applied to his own use of words.

In a talk at the Art Gallery of Hamilton in February 1973, Colville made a number of basic personal observations:

□ Realists are primarily, or initially, concerned with content.

□ A realist is fundamentally interested in experience and giving voice to experience.

□ I don't think realists, by and large, are interested in art as play. The conception of art as puzzles and manipulations of shapes is not fundamental to artists who are called realists. This is not to say that realists do not have some formal preoccupation.

□ I am concerned with space in a controlled way. I think I feel I am very much preoccupied with the problem of time. If you are concerned with the passage of time, you have to be concerned with space in a controlled way.

□ My work has involved my wife to a considerable extent. Anyone working in art uses the life of other people, which is a humbling thought. [Colville's wife appears with him in a large percentage of his paintings.]

In 1963 Colville wrote in the introduction to a realist exhibition, *New Images From Canada,* held at the Banfer Gallery:

Many artists in a developing but essentially pioneer country like Canada have a tendency to want to prove that they can be conventionally *avant-garde,* and therefore not provincial. The artists in this exhibition have the courage and inner direction to be what they are and to do what they think they should do. This, of course, guarantees nothing but sincerity and good intentions; the real question is: "Are the paintings and drawings good?" I think they are, in various ways, the realist tradition being many-faceted, and to various degrees, some of the artists being more mature than others. All I can say in the end is that if they were horses, I would bet on them.

The evidence now in proves that Alex Colville would easily have won his bet. The high level of realism in Canada today owes much to him as spokesman and artist. His stubborn pursuit of realism and mastery of it has helped nourish the ambitions and talents of many of Canada's finest contemporary painters.

Boy, Dog and the Saint John River
Oil and resin on masonite 1958 24 x 32
London Public Library and Art Museum

Stop for Cows
Acrylic on masonite 1967 24 x 36
Fischer Fine Art Limited, London

Ken Danby

Ken Danby has enjoyed the quickest rise to international attention of any Canadian realist. By the age of thirty, he was already represented by major galleries in New York, Paris and Berlin, and his exceptionally large egg-tempera paintings have commanded the attention of both museums and collectors, for the robust authority of their execution and the brisk freshness of their conception.

Danby was born in 1940 at Sault Ste. Marie, Ontario. His father, an assessment commissioner for the city, was descended from Canadian stock as far back as family records were kept. His English-born mother had lived in Sault Ste. Marie since she was nine. With such a background, it is not surprising that Danby is stubbornly attached to the Canadian soil and people as his themes. He is pleased with the international notice he has received, but he insists, "I never want to be known as anything but a Canadian painter."

Ken Danby grew up in a household where the arts were considered important. His father owned a number of paintings, and his mother, who was active in local theatricals, encouraged both Ken and his older brother, Marvin, in their efforts to draw. As is the case with many artists, his special talents emerged early. At the age of ten he won a prize in the local hobby show for a portrait of his father. At eleven he learned about the Ontario College of Art in Toronto from a school guidance counsellor, and determined he would go there – an ambition he realized in 1958, at the age of eighteen.

Danby enjoyed his first year at the Ontario College of Art where he concentrated on drawing constantly, in class and out. When he couldn't find models, he did self-portraits or sketched his own hands and feet. During the first summer from College he worked on a construction gang, building mining towers at the small Ontario community of Wawa. Off shift, he "played at Group of Seven," drawing the local scenery and filling sketchbooks with pen-and-ink drawings of bunkhouse life. These early drawings already reveal his descriptive abilities and eye for the dramatic detail – valuable assets for a future realist.

During his second year at the Art College, Ken learned much from Jock Macdonald. Though Danby's own direction at the time was toward realism, Macdonald instilled in him a respect and tolerance for many different styles of art, from abstract to surrealist. Danby was frustrated by the College's strong emphasis on applied design, however, rather than drawing and painting, and at the end of his second year he decided to leave permanently.

When he returned to Sault Ste. Marie that summer, he worked at a local television station, designing sets, and prepared floats for the annual Community Night Parade. He was permitted to use a shack be-

At the Crease
Egg tempera on masonite 1972 28x40
Collection: Mr Fred Eaton

Detail of *At the Crease*

hind the TV studio for painting, and there began that series of abstract compositions – inspired by the example of Jock Macdonald – which were to occupy him for the next three years.

In the fall Danby returned to Toronto to test his talents in that highly competitive market place. He began a series of jobs which included set painting for a television station (six months), preparing window displays for a women's-wear shop (two weeks), designing packaging for boxes and wrappers (four months). Finally, in the fall of 1961, he found employment as a layout artist for the Toronto *Telegram*, and there he stayed for two years.

Away from work, Danby lived the usual Bohemian life of a young, single artist. He moved from place to place, always painting abstracts. He roomed for more than a year above a Yonge Street cigar store called Benny's, stayed for the winter of 1961-62 over a folk-singing club called The Gate of Cleves, moved after a few months to another folk-singing café known as The Fifth Peg. During that period, Danby had his first one-man exhibition at the local Jack Pollock Gallery, in November of 1961, and managed to sell four abstract paintings. He also won a prize for one of his paintings at a Toronto outdoor exhibition.

The most important event in Danby's evolution as an artist came late in 1962. While returning to Toronto from a New York visit, he detoured to Buffalo's Albright Knox Gallery to see a large one-man exhibition of paintings by realist Andrew Wyeth. There he came face to face with such Wyeth masterpieces as *Miss Olsom, Young Bull, Ground Hog Day, Raccoon, Soaring,* and *Christina's World.* The impact made by these paintings convinced Danby that he should forsake abstract painting, which he was becoming increasingly dissatisfied with, and return completely to his early devotion to realism. Wyeth's success proved to him that realist painting during the 1960's was not a totally underground movement. Furthermore, although he had not done any realist paintings for several years, Danby had continued to draw from nature, which made his return relatively easy.

Danby's first realist painting, *Fur and Bricks,* a composition portraying his cat, Kimbo, walking along the ledge of a roof top, was completed late in 1963. It was his first painting in egg-tempera, a medium he has used ever since.

Fur and Bricks brought Danby his first major recognition when it won a coveted Jessie Dow award at the 1964 Spring Exhibition of the Montreal Museum of Fine Arts. This award, founded in 1908, had been previously won by such noted artists as A.Y.Jackson, Maurice Cullen, J.W.Morrice, Clarence Gagnon, William Brymner, F.M.Suzôr-Coté and Albert Robinson.

The Red Wagon
Egg tempera on masonite   1966   42 x 32
Private Collection

At this time Danby went in search of a dealer, and was accepted by Walter Moos, whose gallery has represented him ever since. The first of his annual realist exhibitions was held at the gallery in 1964. That same year the National Gallery of Canada bought one of his drawings, and later the Gallery purchased a tempera, *Early Morning* (1965). Danby is now represented in such collections as the Museum of Modern Art, New York; the Indianapolis Museum; the Bradford City Art Gallery, England; the Montreal Museum of Fine Arts; the Vancouver Art Gallery; the Mendel Gallery, Saskatoon; and those of United States Steel, the Pittsburgh National Bank, the Toronto-Dominion Bank, and the Power Corporation of Canada.

Many of Danby's paintings for his first Moos Gallery exhibition were conceived on St. Joseph's Island in Lake Huron near Sault Ste Marie. There, in 1964, in the small village of Richard's Landing, he painted a series of watercolours and a number of studies for later tempera paintings. During the next few years, while living in Toronto, he returned to paint on St. Joseph's Island each summer. Those were the years when he established his early reputation for strongly lit, luminous studies of rural Ontario.

Danby's exhibitions from 1964 to 1970 were dominated by rustic themes, and he became associated in the public mind with such nostalgic subjects as barns, rail fences, mills, farmhouses and silos. He painted barnyard cats and boys cycling on country roads or sitting in stubble fields. His paintings of those years bore such titles as *The Ice House* (1970), *Horse Collars* (1967), *At the Feed Mill* (1967), *The Last Pumpkins* (1970), *The Bucket* (1968) and *Weathered Clapboard* (1969). The best of them included *Early Morning* (1965 – National Gallery of Canada), *The Mill Cat* (1968), *Towards the Hill* (1967) and *The Red Wagon* (1966). These were the sort of Danby pictures *Time* magazine described in 1966 as "crumbs of comfort shorn from a home-baked loaf." (In April 1968, Danby painted a portrait of Prime Minister Trudeau for the cover of the same magazine.)

Although most of the subject matter of his paintings was thus closely related during those years of 1964-70, Danby's art continually grew in originality and technical command. He came to handle the difficult egg-tempera medium with an almost virtuoso dexterity. Few artists have wrought from it such a remarkable variety of technical variations, from the softest blendings to almost staccato textures.

Since December 1966, Danby and his wife, Judy, and their two sons have lived at Armstrong's Mill, a historic eleven-acre property a few miles from the city of Guelph. The mill was built in 1830, and the nine-room farmhouse in 1850. Danby paints in a separate studio building

The Mill Cat
Egg tempera on masonite   1968   18 x 25
Collection: Mr and Mrs A. Green

Grooming
Dry brush watercolour   1968   13 x 22
Private Collection

Flat Bottom
Egg tempera on masonite 1972 14 x 20
Collection: Miss Audrey Miller

Snooker
Egg tempera on masonite 1972 22 x 32
Private Collection

Study for *Snooker*
Pencil 1972 21 x 27
Collection: Mr Philip Zierler

on the property. During his periods of peak production, he works from eight in the morning until late at night, but he breaks between five and eight o'clock to spend an uninterrupted interval with his family.

In 1968, Danby did a study of a young man on a motorcycle called *Pulling Out,* one of the first of a series of dramatic contemporary portraits which were to emerge in the 1970's. Although by now he was immersed in the heart of rural Ontario, Danby felt the need to create subject matter outside the world of barns, wells and millstones. He first turned his attention to the neighbouring city of Guelph and found his new material among its teen-agers. The resulting dramatic portraits, *Snooker* (1972), *Delicious* (1972) and *Sharpshooter* (1972) represent subjects which are at once contemporary and ageless in their intense concentration. These are the creative descendants of those dramatic studies of humanity which began earlier with *Pulling Out* (1968), *Reflections* (1970), *Armstrong Miller* (1970) and *His MGB* (1971). One of the finest paintings of the early 1970's, *Motel* (1972), conveys the human condition without human presence. It depicts a crumpled pillow, a telephone, ashtray and plastic coffee cup – summing up all the paraphernalia of the travelling man's morning. It was pictures like *Motel, Delicious* and *Snooker* that won Danby's work wide attention when they were shown at New York's William Zierler Gallery in February 1972.

The masculine power of Danby's realism finds its full force of expression in his portrayal of a goalkeeper, *At the Crease* (1972). This painting represents the egg-tempera technique at its most complex and his imagery at its most compelling. In this anonymous masked presence he entraps the special loneliness of the net-minder. With all his grotesque protection – his pads, gloves, mask and stick – the man is still alone and vulnerable. (Danby is an avid hockey fan, and presented every member of Canada's national hockey team that defeated Russia in 1972 with a copy of his serigraph, *Skates.*) *At the Crease* is creative-miles from the bucolic farmyard scenes of a few years earlier. It is a painting that confirms Danby's growing stature as a truly major realist painter.

Motel
Egg tempera on masonite 1972 16 x 24
Private Collection

Sunbather
Egg tempera on masonite 1972 22 x 32
Private Collection

The Dreamer
Lithograph 1972 23 x 19 (Edition of 100)
Diverse Collections

Delicious
Egg tempera on masonite 1972 24 x 32
William Zierler Gallery, New York

Popcorn
Dry brush watercolour 1972 13-1/2 x 22
William Zierler Gallery, New York

Tom Forrestall

As a child, Tom Forrestall happened to pick up some old books on Titian and Rembrandt which lay about the house. He leafed through them, and determined then and there to be a painter. Encouraged in this ambition by his father, a carpenter and an excellent draughtsman, who drew for his own pleasure, Tom never wavered in this decision.

Though he was born in the Annapolis Valley, at Middleton, Nova Scotia, in 1936, Tom moved to the town of Dartmouth when he was seven. From there he made a trip every Saturday morning to Halifax to attend the children's art classes at the Nova Scotia College of Art. For him the opportunity to work under formal direction more than made up for the play hours he missed. In those classes he learned the basic elements of still-life painting and perspective drawing. And at home he painted landscapes in oil, to take to the art college for criticism.

That early training provided an important foundation for Forrestall's later years at Mount Allison where, at the age of eighteen, he enrolled in the Fine Arts course. For the almost indigent young artist, the university years were a combination of academic pleasure and hard labour. In the classroom Tom studied under Alex Colville, Lawren P. Harris and Edward Pulford. In the evenings and on weekends he worked at washing dishes, cleaning floors, lettering signs, and occasionally baby-sitting for the Colvilles. During the summers, he returned to Middleton, where his father had resettled, and tended the local graveyard. The cemetery later served as the subject of some of his most evocative paintings, including *Their Memory* (1966).

At the end of his graduating year, in September 1958, Tom married a fellow student at Mount Allison, Natalie LeBlanc. The couple went to the Continent for the following year, to study the great art of the European museums. It proved to be an experience which Forrestall considers one of the most useful of his career.

When he returned from abroad Forrestall worked for a year as assistant curator of the Beaverbrook Art Gallery in Fredericton, a city that was to be his base for the next thirteen years. Then a close friend of Lord Beaverbrook's, publisher Brigadier Michael Wardell, hired Tom as editorial cartoonist for the Fredericton *Daily Gleaner* and as designer for the University of New Brunswick Press. An enthusiast for Forrestall's painting, Wardell also made it possible for the artist to buy a six-suite apartment house – an old bakery which had been converted. There Forrestall gave art classes each Wednesday night in a room lined with antique bread ovens.

With money coming in from these classes, from rents and from cartooning, Forrestall could complete his paintings at leisure. Previously he had been forced, by lack of time and security, to paint quickly in oils,

River Valley
Egg tempera on masonite   1971   26 x 26
Roberts Gallery, Toronto

East Coast
Egg tempera on masonite 1971 28x61
Collection: Mr Bobby Orr

Wedding in the Valley
Egg tempera on masonite 1971 18x41
Roberts Gallery, Toronto

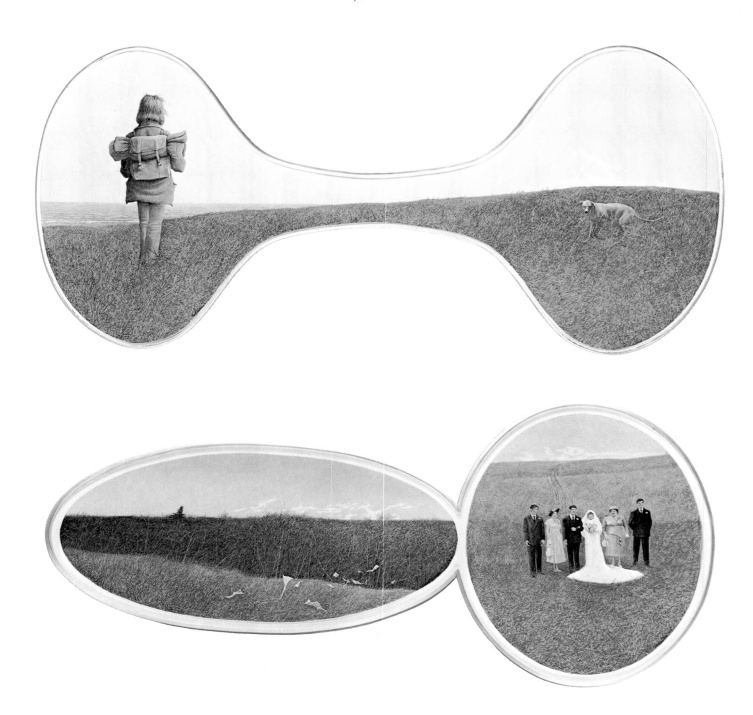

a method which he has described as "just a matter of squeezing the tube." Now he was able to adopt the slower technique of egg tempera, alternating with acrylics, a method more suited to the detailed and deliberate sort of realist paintings he was ambitious to produce.

In 1963 Forrestall rented a summer house at Tatamagouche, on New Brunswick's north shore. There he worked full time for almost a month, finishing a few large acrylic paintings and a number of water-colours. At that time he began the practice of doing dozens of sketches in the field and taking them back to his studio for study. If he feels a subject has further creative potential, he will return to the site and make an additional series of detailed notes from it. Frequently, when examining a group of sketches, he will find two or three which harmo-niously fit together into a set for multiple-shape compositions.

Outdoor sketching represents a vital part of Forrestall's method as an artist. He rarely uses photographs, since he feels a personal need to renew pictorial experience slowly from reality. "Nothing can replace that," he says. He also enjoys the act of field sketching, which he com-pares to going fishing. To mount his pictorial catches, he uses trans-parent watercolour, inks and pastels, on Strathmore board. He rarely spends more than an hour on a watercolour.

By 1967 Forrestall was using egg tempera exclusively as his medium for major studio works. Until then, from 1963, he had alternated be-tween plastic acrylic paints and the centuries-old tempera. He finally decided on tempera, he says, because of its luminosity and opalescence. He also feels that the natural constituents of egg tempera give it an organic character, both in appearance and use, and finds the handling and effects of acrylic comparatively harsh. His choice of medium was confirmed after examining the originals of Italian fifteenth-century masters, whose paintings in tempera on gesso remain as brilliant today as when they were painted, whereas oils on canvas darken with time.

Like other high realists, Forrestall has had to fight against a tide of abstract and pop art which was particularly strong during the 1960's. Official art circles, so often prone to follow international fashion's dictates, virtually ignored the work of the high realists, who have won their ground with little public support other than that supplied by re-gional institutions. By 1962 Forrestall's painting was beginning to receive some recognition, however. In that year, the University of New Brunswick gave him his first one-man show. And following that his work was included in numerous important group and individual exhi-bitions – at the University of Western Ontario (1964), Roberts Gallery, Toronto (1965), Dartmouth College, New Hampshire (1966), and the Walter Klinkhoff Gallery, Montreal (1967).

In Blakney's Field
Egg tempera on masonite 1971 33-1/4 x 20
Private Collection

Huge Boulder
Egg tempera on masonite 1972 26-1/2 x 36-3/4
Collection: Mr and Mrs Joseph Dalton

The West Nova Scotians
Egg tempera on masonite 1971 48 x 29
Private Collection

Burning Field
Egg tempera on masonite 1972 14 x 15
Collection: Mr Ted O'Beay

In 1968 he held four one-man exhibitions – at Dalhousie University in Halifax, Roberts Gallery in Toronto, Sir George Williams University in Montreal, and the Morrison Art Gallery in Saint John. These showings brought his work to the attention of museums throughout the country, and his paintings are now included in many prominent collections, including the Art Gallery of Windsor, the Confederation Centre Art Gallery in Charlottetown, the New Brunswick Museum in Saint John, the Winnipeg Art Gallery, Sir George Williams University in Montreal, and the Owens Art Gallery in Sackville. In 1971-72 the Beaverbrook Art Gallery organized a major circulating exhibition of his work which travelled across Canada from Victoria to the Montreal Museum of Fine Arts.

By late 1972 Forrestall's position as an artist was secure enough to enable him to leave the city of Fredericton and return to Dartmouth, the town where he had spent most of his active boyhood and for which he has retained a deep attachment. "I think I feel more at ease there, both creatively and socially, than anywhere," he says. In Dartmouth he bought a vast grey-and-white clapboard house which had once housed the local Y.M.C.A., and he now lives there with his wife and six children. The top floor, one enormous room, functions as his studio, where he paints from nine in the morning until about six in the evening. He usually paints at a traditional easel, using whisky shot glasses as containers for his tempera colours, and a large china meat platter as a mixing palette.

In Forrestall's studio there are usually more than a dozen white gessoed panels of different shapes – triangles, rhomboids, quatrefoils, trifoils, squares, circles, ovals, T-forms – all cut from masonite. These are the bases for his new paintings, awaiting a theme or idea to fill them – individually, in pairs, or even in sets of three. Forrestall rarely uses rectangular boards for his paintings, preferring the challenge of varied shapes. He has experimented with these unusual forms since 1961, and now uses them almost exclusively.

Forrestall is surprised when his shapes are described as *avant garde* or as novelties. Circular, oval, rhomboid, and other configurations have been used to "frame" works of art from classical times. They are often found in ancient Mediterranean, Celtic, and Italian art. The diptych and triptych were commonplace for Renaissance and Romanesque artists. Forrestall is simply continuing a long tradition, and adding a fresh, contemporary point of view to it.

He does not pretend to be able to apply logic to his combinations of visual shapes. Forms are often brought together for the purpose of establishing a mood, as in *The West Nova Scotians*, or to hint at a continuum of experience, as in *Two Weeks* (1971) where three related diamond-shaped panels contain a self portrait, a rumpled bed and panes of glass reflecting a winter landscape. Sometimes Forrestall views a landscape through two related circular panels, as though looking at it through binoculars. The focus and perspective are retained as the normal eye would simultaneously view them. At other times he will make sudden, dramatic changes in scale in his paired panels, as in *Visiting Day*, where the eye is forced into a sudden switch of focus. This relates closely to the split-screen technique in modern cinematography; though he rarely uses a camera, Forrestall acknowledges the impact of contemporary photography upon his art.

Forrestall normally spends a long time studying pictorial combinations before arriving at one that interests him, though occasionally he will see a theme which instantly demands a particular shape or combination of shapes. Recently he has considered doing a related series of "shape" pictures, portraying the same subject – say a pine tree – from many points of view, literally bringing his theme to a full circle.

Visiting Day
Egg tempera on masonite 1971 30 x 31
Collection: Miss Edith Townsend

Detail of *Visiting Day*

Best and Company
Egg tempera on masonite 1970 14 x 14
Collection: Mr and Mrs R.B. Hillary

Eric Freifeld

Eric Freifeld is the only major high realist in Canada who paints exclusively in traditional transparent watercolours. Within the limits imposed by this technique, he has created haunting pictorial comments about the transience of human existence and the man-made material world.

Born in Saratov, Russia, in 1919, Freifeld emigrated to Western Canada with his widowed mother, an older sister and his nurse, in 1924. In Edmonton he was brought up by the nanny, an old family friend, while his mother worked as a public health nurse in the District of Peers, a five-hour train ride north of the city. In the thirteen years she worked as an outpost nurse, Eric seldom saw his mother except during the summer months. As a result he was forced to develop his own emotional resources, and his inner need to do creative work was accentuated.

While attending elementary and high school Eric continually painted in his spare time. From the age of fourteen, he was doing street scenes of Edmonton, inspired by books from the public library about British watercolour painters. At sixteen he quit school with his mother's permission to concentrate full time on painting. This decision was confirmed when, at seventeen, he won a Canada-wide Carnegie Trust Competition to attend the Banff Summer School of Fine Arts. There he produced a multitude of small monochrome landscape compositions, almost abstract in design. To this day he makes it a practice to see everything in abstract terms before beginning to draw.

When he returned from Banff Freifeld continued painting Edmonton scenes while working as an usher at the local Rialto cinema. It took all of his determination to maintain the ambition to be a professional artist. He had very little money and saw virtually no original art to sustain him. (The occasional travelling art show which came from Eastern Canada seemed "overwhelming" and he longed one day to go East.) His first youthful exhibition at the Hudson Bay Company received no reviews and no sales. A second one-man show at Edmonton's Macdonald Hotel, early in 1938, netted him about two hundred dollars. A few months later he took that money and a few more dollars he had saved, and set out to achieve his ambition to go East and to Europe. From Edmonton to Toronto he travelled as a paid attendant on a cattle train. From there he hitch-hiked to Montreal and hired on as a cattle-boat hand for a twelve-day trip to Glasgow.

In Scotland Freifeld eagerly sought out the fine art galleries of Glasgow and Edinburgh, and then hitch-hiked to London. For the next year, working from a room near Waterloo Station, Freifeld made London his base. He found the great city hospitable to his needs and

Ichabod
Watercolour 1950 21 x 29
Collection: The Artist

The MacNeil Place
Watercolour 1964 22-3/4 x 30-3/4
Collection: The Artist

talents. He enrolled in night classes at St. Martin's School of Art to study figure drawing, and painted London street scenes during the day. London offered him limitless resources in galleries, acquaintances and visual themes. The atmosphere gave him courage, and soon after he arrived he submitted a watercolour entitled *Prelude, Vancouver,* to the famed New English Art Club. It was accepted for hanging alongside exhibits by such famous figures as Augustus John and Paul Nash. This mark of prestige brought Freifeld considerable publicity both in Britain and at home. Even the *Edmonton Bulletin* ran an editorial on the young artist's success.

The New English Art Club acceptance also brought Freifeld an invitation to show at London's prestigious Brooks Street Gallery. The gallery advanced him expenses to paint for six weeks in southern France during the winter of 1938-39, and in February of 1939 exhibited fourteen of his paintings done around Cannes, along with twenty-five Canadian and British subjects. The show's titles offered a cosmopolitan mixture of titles: *Yachts at Cannes; Thames Embankment; Coal Harbour, Vancouver* and *Ice-house, Alberta.* Reviews of the Brooks Street exhibit were invariably favourable. The London *Times* critic, Eric Newton, commented, "He composes well; he has an exceedingly good sense of tone, so that he is able to apply his colours firmly and directly, and his handling of the medium is broad and free." The London show was a complete sell-out.

Freifeld returned to Canada in the summer of 1939, and divided his time for the next few years between Edmonton and Vancouver. He was given his first museum one-man exhibition by the Vancouver Art Gallery in 1940, from which he sold a few paintings. A second exhibition at Edmonton's Macdonald Hotel a few months later sold nothing. Freifeld wondered at the contrast between his instant success in London, a world art centre, and his failure in his home town, where he was now reduced to working as a salesman in a women's shoe store.

In 1942 his financial problems were solved when he enlisted in the Canadian Army. After basic training, he was picked to join a small specialized group of camouflage artists stationed in Vancouver. Most of the duties involved were of a creative nature, and for three months Freifeld worked with Jack Shadbolt on a mural for the local United Services Centre. During the 1942-43 school season, he was permitted to teach evening classes in drawing and painting at the Vancouver School of Art.

Freifeld's work up until this time had been freely drawn, broadly painted, sometimes almost expressionistic watercolours. They were spirited and summary in character and made little attempt at close

definition. Not until he enlisted in the Army did Freifeld reveal the
penetrating analysis of form which foretold his eventual career in
closely wrought realism. But by the early 1940's his carefully defined
pencil drawings of Vancouver's Chinatown and of individual structures such as *The Old Gravel Mill* (1943) showed evidences of his eventual sustained, detailed style.

In 1944, following his discharge, Freifeld went to New York to study
at the Art Students' League on a veteran's grant. During his two years
there he divided his time between life classes at the League and painting the structural face of the city – the sort of places he has since continued to portray. Indeed, old houses and streets have concerned
Freifeld as an artist since boyhood. Whether he has painted them in
Edmonton, Vancouver, Cannes, London, New York or Toronto, he
has found in them parables relating to humanity. Some of his works –
Ichabod (1950) and *Gomorrah* (1951), for example – relate imagined
biographies of buildings to biblical stories. During the year 1948, while
ill at the Hamilton Mountain Sanitarium, he reflected the aridity of
institutional life in such compositions as *Sanitarium* (1948).

Freifeld's paintings, like his themes, have taken on a deeper character of their own with the years. His art is concerned with the relationship between man's life and the fleeting passage of time. Almost all of
his fifteen major works are related, using objects to symbolize a space
which has been lived in, shared, abused or loved. Most of his subjects
have been found in downtown Toronto, or the surrounding southern
Ontario countryside.

Freifeld's technique has naturally evolved out of his themes and
what he has to say about them. He uses the aging cracks in sidewalks,
tilted slate roofs, leaning verandah pillars, decaying wallpaper and jut-
ting laths to make his philosophical comment. No Canadian artist has
ever drawn with more subtlety or more sustained emotion than
Freifeld has in such a technical *tour-de-force* as *Roses Are Red* (1964 –
Montreal Museum of Fine Arts), *Alfred's Room* (1967 – Vancouver Art
Gallery), *Pauline* (1966), or *Tutt's Barn* (1963).

Although he has taught at the Ontario College of Art since 1946,
Freifeld has managed to create a body of distinguished and original
works, divided between large, patiently rendered compositions which
sometimes require years to complete, to dramatic, on-the-spot studies.
His medium is invariably a combination of transparent watercolour
washes and carbon pencil drawing. His broad watercolour studies are
done on the spot in a matter of hours, but his studio compositions are
done, on and off, over a period of years. He begins them before the
subject, and develops them later, slowly and deliberately, taking what-

Back Door
Watercolour 1954 21-1/2 x 30
Collection: Mr Ron MacDonald

104

ever liberties he believes necessary with perspective or proportion, to underline the dramatic realism of his subjects. To control the tonal subtleties of his delicate washes he always works by daylight.

In 1971 Freifeld wrote a statement about his painting *Roses Are Red,* which sums up his own creative philosophy: "To ask what my painting *Roses Are Red* means is tantamount to asking the meaning of my entire work, since it is one of a series of about fifteen sustained works. Each picture is a variation on the same basic theme which deals with the life cycle, and my constant and continuous curiosity about the why and wherefore of life and death – it always intrigues me that people come and go, but things seem to last longer and outlive people.

"In *Roses Are Red* my subject is an abandoned, decaying farmhouse and its contents. It speaks of the lives of the people who lived there and all the associations of those lives. . . . The deepest sense I felt was a sadness at man's mortality. . . . An artist loves objects, and I was moved by the knowledge that the objects here, associated with a man's life, faded and disintegrated, still retained their symbolic weight and evocative powers."

About his own creative direction Freifeld says, "I have not evolved a system of images or symbols, and there is no attempt in my work to stage ritual order. My pictures deal with the mundane, the unarranged and the accidental. In this and other ways I am a realist."

As a realist, Freifeld has been almost careless of public acclaim. He has patiently pursued his special world of ordered ruin – a pursuit hardly gauged to attain instant popularity. In fact, he is so reluctant to release his works for sale that he describes pictures by him in museums as "unfinished." Despite this refusal to join in the current popularity sweepstakes, Freifeld has emerged as one of the significant painters of his generation.

Roses are Red
Watercolour 1964 27-1/2 x 40
Montreal Museum of Fine Arts

Detail of *Roses are Red*

E. J. Hughes

E.J.Hughes has been one of the major pioneers of detailed realism in Canada. For more than forty years he has stubbornly pursued his own road toward a strikingly personal style of realist art and from the details of the Pacific coast landscape has composed a pristine and carefully rendered world.

Edward John Hughes has always lived near the Pacific. Born in Vancouver in 1913, he spent his childhood in the city of Nanaimo, on the east coast of Vancouver Island. There he grew up close to the busy harbour, with its steamers, barges, wharves and inlets – the very stuff from which his most memorable paintings are created.

His interest in drawing began as a child in Nanaimo and continued after his family returned to Vancouver when he was ten. His father, a professional musician who played the trombone in a number of Vancouver theatre orchestras, encouraged him to study, and he took lessons from a local painter, Mrs. Verrall. Even then his drawings revealed an inclination toward realism.

Hughes was only sixteen when he enrolled at the Vancouver School of Art in 1929. He was fortunate in his instructors at the school, who included J.W.G.(Jock) Macdonald and F.H.Varley, two of the finest teachers and painters in Canada. Macdonald, who had been originally trained as a textile designer in Scotland, strengthened his natural bent for strong patterns, which reveals itself in all his later paintings.

By his twenties, Hughes possessed a ready command of realist painting techniques. A portrait of his mother painted in 1939 is almost fifteenth-century Flemish in its attention to detail, particularly in its fastidious treatment of a tapestry behind the head of the sitter.

After six years of study Hughes began to earn his living doing a variety of commercial art projects around Vancouver. He joined forces with two other realists, Paul Goranson and Orville Fisher, and with them was involved in many large mural projects, including the wall decorations for the British Columbia exhibit at the San Francisco Fair of 1939. Hughes' talent for design was a valuable asset for such assignments, and he produced many murals, including panels for local restaurants, hotels and pubs, as well as one for the Vancouver First United Church.

In September 1939 Hughes enlisted in the Royal Canadian Artillery. Following initial training as a gunner, he acted as a non-commissioned army artist until early in 1942, when he was appointed an Official War Artist. For the next four and a half years he served in Canada, Kiska, Alaska and Great Britain, recording army manoeuvres and operations. Not every painter excelled as a war artist, but Hughes' skills as a draughtsman, his realist style, and his industrious nature made him an

The Beach Southeast of Crofton
Oil on canvas 1973 25 x 32
Dominion Gallery, Montreal

Beach at Savary Island, B.C.
Oil on canvas 1952 20 x 24
National Gallery of Canada

Stanley Park
Pencil c.1946 8 x 12
Collection: Mr Ron MacDonald

Finlayson Arms
Oil on canvas 1965 32 x 48
Dominion Gallery, Montreal

ideal choice. During those years he produced more than five hundred drawings and paintings – a remarkable achievement considering the difficult conditions under which he frequently worked.

Following his discharge in the summer of 1946, Hughes went to Victoria where he joined his wife, the former Fern Smith, whom he had married in 1940. The first peacetime paintings contained the same strong element of design evident in the war studies, but added a new rich quality of texture, prompted by the landscape along the coast and the artist's own affection for pictorial minutiae.

Hughes has always been fascinated by visual details, and his paintings often include close-ups: bark, shingles, lichen, fern fronds. The works done between 1946 and 1951, in particular, possess an almost tapestry-like build-up of textural effects. Waves and clouds seem almost modelled in relief. With such a painstaking approach, it is not surprising that he produced no more than four or five pictures each year during that period. This preoccupation with texture is particularly evident in *Farm Near Courtenay, B.C.* (1949 – Vancouver Art Gallery), which is almost Brueghel-like in its affectionate matter-of-fact rendering of the earth and its harvest.

The sea is present in almost all of Hughes' paintings, frequently dotted by fishing boats, tugs and coastal steamers belching smoke. This is true of *Ladysmith Harbour* (1949 – Art Gallery of Ontario), *Steamer Arriving at Nanaimo* (1950) and *Entrance to Howe Sound* (1949).

The immediate post-war years were trying ones for Hughes financially. He concentrated solely on his paintings, each of which required months to complete, and sales were very far apart. To economize, he moved from Victoria in 1951 to Shawnigan, a lakeside community about thirty miles north of Victoria. There he found another benefit – isolation from the activities of a large city, and the peace and quiet needed by most high realists.

It was in Shawnigan that Hughes was discovered by Montreal's Dominion Gallery director, Dr. Max Stern, who agreed to buy all of his future output. Since then, all of the artist's work has been channelled through the one gallery and his production of paintings has increased to an average of one per month. His first one-man exhibition was held at the Dominion Gallery in 1954.

Since 1951, Hughes' work has been less intensely involved with textural effects. His surfaces are smoother, with an increasing clarity of colour. *The Beach at Savary Island* (1952 – National Gallery of Canada), *Howe Sound* (1955) and *Beach Southeast of Crofton* (1973) illustrate his progress towards a more simplified stylistic approach, with larger open areas of space and colour.

Trees, Sooke Harbour, B.C.
Oil on canvas   1951   30 x 24
Collection: Dr and Mrs Max Stern

The seeming simplicity of Hughes' hard-edged realism is the result of a carefully honed technique, long effort and a thorough knowledge of art history. His approach to painting is workmanlike and deliberate. He utilizes the entire second floor of his Shawnigan house as a studio, and his creative methods are as orderly as one might expect from such a meticulous craftsman.

The source material for Hughes' canvases are exact, on-the-spot pencil drawings upon which he has written careful notations describing the colours of specific areas and objects. For the final paintings he uses traditional oil-painting materials and techniques, working at an easel from a hand-held palette.

E.J. Hughes' patient evolution as an artist was recognized in 1967 by a major one-man retrospective show at the Art Gallery of Vancouver and York University, Toronto. Organized by Vancouver Gallery director Doris Shadbolt, the exhibition of fifty works revealed Hughes as a unique and important Canadian artist.

Entrance to Howe Sound
Oil on canvas 1949 32 x 36
Collection: Mr Ron MacDonald

Ernest Lindner

Ernest Lindner may fairly be called a pioneer of Canadian high realism. Born in 1897, he has pursued a realist path for more than forty years.

Lindner's dedication to creative craftsmanship began as a youth in his native Vienna. His father and grandfather were manufacturers of hand-fashioned walking sticks and parasols, with a continent-wide reputation for design. The apartment in which Ernest grew up with his twelve brothers and sisters was located above the family workshop, where specialized woodworkers, sculptors and jewellers laboured to create the quality Lindner products. During the day, Ernest attended the state high school, where he received a thorough training in academic drawing, but in his spare hours he haunted the workshop, watching the master craftsmen and occasionally trying his own hand at wood-turning or sketching a design for an ornamented handle. His drawing even then was in the direction of forest fantasies, a thematic preoccupation which was never to leave him.

Ernest's apprenticeship in his father's business was cut short by the outbreak of World War I. He was not yet eighteen when he enlisted in a mountaineer regiment of the Austrian army, and he did not return home to stay until after the German defeat in the fall of 1918. During those years he had little opportunity to draw, but did manage, while recuperating from battle wounds in 1917, to do a number of pen-and-ink studies, including a remarkably detailed rendering of the family home in Vienna.

With the return of peace, Lindner worked in a number of brokerage houses and banks in various parts of Austria. At the time he was fascinated by the world of finance. Inflation was rampant, and he enjoyed the excitement of currency speculation which then dominated his work. In 1924 he returned briefly to the family business at the urging of two older brothers who now ran it with their father. Ernest's natural art talents were needed to design walking sticks and umbrellas, and he did so well at it that he won a gold medal at a Stuttgart industrial fair the same year. Still restless for financial adventure, he purchased a candy factory with his two brothers as partners, a venture that was quickly bankrupted by the same currency speculation that had earlier occupied him. In the spring of 1926, broke and dispirited, he decided to leave the ruins of Europe and try his luck in Canada. "I had nothing to lose," he now recalls, "and as it turned out a great deal to gain."

Immigration into Canada was then severely restricted, and the only way the twenty-nine-year-old Lindner could gain entry was to sign on as a farm worker bound for Saskatchewan. Upon his arrival, he was located at the small settlement of Markinch, north of Regina. He re-

Deep in the Woods
Watercolour 1967 28 x 20
National Gallery of Canada

The Fledgling
Watercolour 1968 29 x 21
Collection: Mr and Mrs G.P. Wigle

mained there for the summer and autumn, but moved for the winter to Saskatoon where, existing on his small savings, he began his first Canadian landscapes. The sunlit pastel, *Saskatchewan Farmyard* (1926), belongs to this era. Lindner worked one more summer in the fields, at Twelve Mile Lake in southern Saskatchewan, before settling permanently in Saskatoon. He soon found that he had arrived in the prairie city at a difficult time, however, just ahead of the great depression and the devastating droughts of the late 1920's. But he managed to survive by working for the first few years as a house painter and decorator. He supplemented his income by infrequent freelance work as a commercial artist, producing illustrations for ads, letterheads and business cards for local printing houses.

Lindner, who was then a bachelor, spent every hour he could spare from earning a livelihood drawing and painting. "I concentrated on art," he has said, "because I was very lonesome." From this difficult period of adjustment came a number of telling portraits, including *Old Salesman* (1929), a study redolent of the depression atmosphere. Even more stark were his drawings commissioned to illustrate *Man: Jungle-wise and Other-wise* by John McNaughton, a local author. These he produced in his apartment-studio in an office block, the London Building, which remained his headquarters for more than a dozen years.

In 1931 Saskatoon inaugurated a Technical Collegiate Institute, and Lindner obtained part-time employment as a night school teacher, his first regular work since settling in Canada. By 1935 he was hired as a day teacher, the only full-time art instructor in the Saskatoon school system. He continued as a teacher and eventually department head until his retirement in 1962.

In his decades of teaching, Lindner had an immeasurable impact upon the early development of art on the prairies. With a free hand to evolve his own academic programme, he created an atmosphere that encouraged community involvement both within and without the collegiate. His graduates down the years included many noteworthy artists. One of them, Ted Pulford, went on to instruct at Mount Allison University, where he in turn taught other important high realists Christopher Pratt, Tom Forrestall and D.P. Brown.

By the time he retired, Lindner had completely evolved his highly personal style and concept of realist painting. With the aid of photography, he began in the early 1960's to execute the astonishing close-ups of tree trunks and vegetation which are his hallmark. Once he began painting full time, Lindner's work showed a dramatic advance in subtlety of drawing, richness of texture and individuality of colour. His one-man exhibition held at New York's Banfer Gallery in 1965

Fungi
Watercolour 1969 29x21
Collection: Mr F.M. Fenton

Castles in the Forest
Pen and ink   1964   21-1/2 x 29-1/2
Collection: The Artist

Hand of the Artist
Watercolour   1966   14-1/2 x 21
Collection: The Artist

revealed an artist who, late in life, had finally arrived at a strikingly original concept of nature. Closing in on the most delicate intricacies of bark, lichen, mould and foliage, his compositions force the spectator to take a fresh look at the forest world at his feet. The twenty-four paintings and drawings in the Banfer Exhibition announced the emergence of one of Canada's most dedicated painters. The noted American critic, Clement Greenberg, aptly commented, "I find more imagination and modernity in Ernest Lindner's sharply focussed rendering of a tree trunk than in the largest part of current abstract painting."

Lindner's modernity represents a kind of high realism arrived at after a life of continual refinement of craftsmanship and creative vision. He eventually came to handle watercolour with a consummate skill equalled only by a few in the history of Canadian painting. Such watercolours as *Deep in the Woods* (1967 – National Gallery of Canada), and *The Fledgling* (1968) are works of sheer virtuosity, and it would be difficult to conceive of a more perfect control of the medium. But whether painting in watercolour, egg tempera or plastic acrylic, and all technique aside, Ernest Lindner has presented us with as unique a pictorial world as that of any Canadian artist. It is not the sort of art that overwhelms with clever tricks of style, but commands attention for its deeply considered and pervasive power of realism.

By the time he was seventy, Lindner's art was finally beginning to receive the wider attention it deserved. One-man museum exhibitions were held at Regina's Norman Mackenzie Gallery (1962), Mendel Art Gallery, Saskatoon (1965, 1968) and the Regina Public Library (1968). In 1970 a major retrospective of eighty-eight works was organized for the Mendel Art Gallery by its director, John Climer.

In his continuing creative search, Lindner launched, in 1969, upon a three-year series of large pencil drawings of what he called "human landscapes." In these he combined his long interest in nature with close-ups of the nude female form, often using repeated and superimposed versions of the same figure. These drawings were shown in seven public art galleries across Canada in 1972. They graphically illustrated Lindner's credo, stated for the catalogue of an exhibition, *Eleven Saskatchewan Artists,* held in 1967: "I paint what I can't say in words. I try to express my thoughts and feelings as I observe life in the forest, on the prairie, in people, everywhere. Life as revealed in the smallest growth is, to me, most meaningful. Forms change, life goes on."

Edge of the Woods
Pen and ink 1964 22-1/2 x 28-1/2
Collection: The Artist

Hugh Mackenzie

The human figure has played a remarkably small part in twentieth-century Canadian painting. Many of our painters have literally not been able to see humanity for the trees. Most major high realists have reversed this direction, however, and their art shows more concern for the figure than for nature. The figure is particularly evident in the work of Hugh Mackenzie whose major compositions have usually centred around nudes or children.

Mackenzie, who was born in Toronto in 1928, spent his early childhood in London, Ontario where his father was manager of a brewery. But he spent his formative years, from eight to fifteen, at Lakefield, a private boarding school near Peterborough, which his father had attended. While there he drew detailed studies of ships, tanks and aeroplanes, but showed little other creative inclination, to the disappointment of his mother who had studied art at Parson's School of Design in New York and was a gifted part-time painter.

Mackenzie decided to be an artist after leaving Lakefield at fifteen, a decision prompted in part by his mother's constant encouragement. He drew continuously for the next three years, which he spent at London's South Collegiate Institute. And at eighteen he enrolled in the Ontario College of Art.

The atmosphere at the College of Art was very different from that of a supervised private school, and Mackenzie found the new self-discipline an exciting challenge. He first learned what painting was all about, he says, "from instructors who cared." These included Carl Schaefer, Jock Macdonald, John Alfsen and Eric Freifeld – all artists noted for their attention to creative craftsmanship and careful technique.

In the summer after graduation, at twenty-two, Mackenzie worked on a construction job to help pay for a year in Paris. From September, he lived in the French capital at the Maison Canadienne, part of University City. With the realization that he had much to learn about drawing, he enrolled for four months at the Grande Chaumière Academy where he drew in pencil from the model almost every day. He says he "enjoyed being miserable and unhappy" in Paris, living on coffee, brandy and cigarettes. He made side trips to visit the museums of Holland, Belgium and Italy. Apart from those visits and the time spent at Grande Chaumière, he now says his period in Paris was creatively "a lost year."

Mackenzie did very little painting for a year after his return to Canada, and in the fall of 1951, having decided he should be an art teacher, he enrolled at Mount Allison University. His two years there proved important to his future. He began to get a sense of technique

Boy with Stilts
Egg tempera on panel 1972 Diameter 10-1/2
Collection: Mr and Mrs Mort Lesser

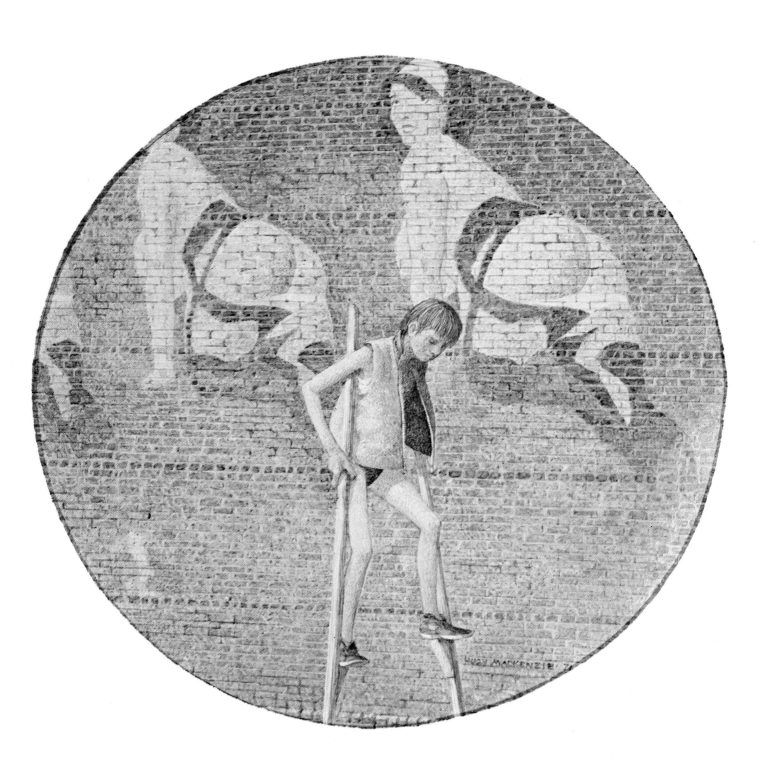

Cogwheel with Flowers
Egg tempera on board   1971   Diameter 6-3/4
Private Collection

Girl on the Couch
Egg tempera on board   1971   Diameter 22
Private Collection

Portrait of Lester B. Pearson (Detail)
Egg tempera on panel   1968
Department of State, Ottawa

through his association with instructors Lawren P. Harris and Alex Colville, who taught drawing and mural painting. Colville, from whom he learned a great deal, introduced him to egg-tempera techniques which he later came to favour for his realist paintings. He received his Bachelor of Fine Arts Degree in 1953, and the following year married Dorothy Johnson, a fellow student at Mount Allison.

After graduation Mackenzie returned to Toronto to teach, but instead found a job for six months doing layouts for a lithography firm. He then briefly became a graphic planner for a consulting engineer, and found that he enjoyed drawing cross-sections and plans for tools. He also painted murals at the Canadian National Exhibition, and eventually obtained a position with the Avro Aircraft Corporation, where his skills as a draughtsman proved invaluable. For three years, from the fall of 1955 to 1958, he worked in Avro's illustration department, drawing projections of planes, charts for pilots' service manuals, advertising brochures and graphs. He found these mechanical renderings a satisfying discipline, and some of the studio techniques he learned then he still uses today. Forced to project complex mechanical designs into pen drawings, he became expert in the intricacies of perspective, and learned to visualize three-dimensional forms in his own head.

Mackenzie believes his three years as a mechanical illustrator deeply affected his future style and themes as a painter. "It is no accident," he says, "that my cars or cogwheels look right, and that I contrast organic and mechanical forms against one another." This is clearly displayed in the paintings *Cogwheel with Flowers* (1971), *Girl and Volkswagen* (1969) and *Egg and Brick* (1968). It is also revealed in his fondness for depicting brick walls, as in the backgrounds for *The Bamboo Poles* (1968), *Boy with Stilts* (1969), *Parking Lot* (1969) and *The Window* (1969). This tendency he shares with the American Ben Shahn, one of his favourite artists.

Valuable though they later may have proved, Mackenzie's three years at Avro saw him produce only one painting, *Modern Madonna* (1957-58), a casein-tempera portrait of his wife feeding their first child, Charles. The picture was accepted for exhibition by the Ontario Society of Artists show in 1958. Encouraged by this, he returned to painting full time, which resulted in a period of financial and personal stress. He forced himself to paint from nine until five each day, composing in the slow casein-tempera technique. But sales were almost non-existent.

By the fall of 1959, with a second child on the way, Mackenzie accepted a job teaching art for a year at Ottawa's High School of Com-

Girl and Volkswagen
Egg tempera on panel 1969 18 x 20
Collection: Mr Ward Cornell

The Window
Egg tempera on panel 1969 21 x 25
Private Collection

Detail of *The Window*

merce. The following year he went to London, Ontario to teach at
H.B.Beal Secondary School. Despite these demands on his time, he
managed to paint enough works between 1958 and 1960 to have a
one-man show at Hart House, University of Toronto, in 1960.

Things now began to fall into place for Mackenzie. He painted
enthusiastically in the evenings, on weekends and during summer holi-
days. In 1961 he won the Ontario Society of Artists' Forster Award for
his tempera, *Woman with Sheet,* and amassed enough works for his first
one-man commercial gallery show, held at Toronto's Jerrold Morris
International Gallery in November 1963. Collectors responded to the
new artist with purchases, and critical response was encouraging. Pearl
McCarthy wrote in the *Globe and Mail,* "His approach to realism is
today's, as is the technique in drawing. It is delightful work, not reac-
tionary academism. So far Canadians have been slow to appreciate this
type of thing and realize its contemporary prompting." In this show he
first exhibited a nude, *Nude with Red Drapery* (1963), a small square
panel, which was to be the first of the many distinguished nudes he was
to do over the next decade, including *Girl and Volkswagen* (1969), *Girl
on the Couch* (1971), *Girl with Sheet* (1969) and *The Staircase* (1969).

Mackenzie continued to teach and paint in London until June 1965,
when he took a year's leave of absence from the classroom. In the summer of 1964 he had begun a large self-portrait, his first painting to be
acquired by a public collection – the Montreal Museum of Fine Arts.
Such recognition made his second one-man show at the Jerrold Morris
Gallery, in October 1966, a sell-out. Creatively, it was a significant exhibition. As well as the large *Self-portrait,* it included many of Mackenzie's
best works, *Mary Climbing the Fence* (1966), *The Highway* (1966), *The Sail*
(1966) and *Portrait of Don* (1966).

By the 1966 show, Mackenzie had perfected his personal egg-
tempera technique, using a subtle combination of light washes and fine
cross-hatching to slowly build his forms. In 1967 he left London for
Toronto (where he has continued to reside since) to teach life classes at
the Ontario College of Art. His best-known and most widely reproduced painting dates from this period – the official portrait of Prime
Minister Lester B. Pearson, which now hangs in Ottawa's Parliament
Buildings. Mackenzie was selected to do the portrait by the Prime
Minister's wife, Maryon Pearson, after she had seen an exhibition of
his work. For three months, from December 1967 until the following
March, he concentrated on this commission. There were no formal sit-
tings for it, and the artist had only a total of about four hours with his
subject during three different visits over a period of a month. During
these sessions Mackenzie took a series of polaroid shots from different

Study for *Girl and Volkswagen*
Charcoal 1969 22 x 15
Private Collection

Study for *The Window*
Pencil 1969 17 x 11
Private Collection

Mary Climbing the Fence
Egg tempera on panel 1966 10 x 12-1/2
Collection: Mr and Mrs Ralph M. Roger

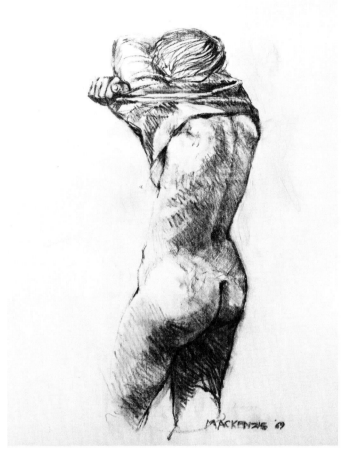

angles, and did a number of quick pencil sketches of the Prime Minister at work, "groping," he says, "for a concept as well as a likeness." He also locked himself in a C.B.C. projection room for hours at a time, studying newsreel footage of the Prime Minister. From all this information, a large charcoal drawing of the final composition was submitted to the Pearsons, and from this the final painting, in egg tempera on masonite panel, was completed. During its execution, Mackenzie made several brief visits to Ottawa to check final colour notes for skin tones. The completed portrait is one of the finest official portraits done in Canada. The artist says, "He had difficult features to paint; it could easily have come out just a pudding face. But it worked out well. He looks like a tough, sensitive and complex man, and he was." Since then, Mackenzie has done a number of selected commissioned portraits, a challenge he enjoys in moderation, and in 1970 he went on a Canada Council grant to England to make a close study of British portraiture.

The Bamboo Poles
Egg tempera on panel 1968 15 x 19
Collection: Mr and Mrs G.A.H. Pearson

Christiane Pflug

The most isolated and singular of Canada's high realists was Christiane Pflug. From the inner domestic world of kitchen and living room, she put forth a memorable and compelling group of canvases. A truly tragic figure, she was the spiritual victim of a cruel war, and her early death was a significant loss to Canadian art.

Christiane's childhood was spent amidst the uncertainties of wartime Germany. She lacked even the security of a family. When her widowed mother enlisted as an army nurse, Christiane was boarded in Kitzbuhel, Austria with an elderly woman who, although unable to supply emotional security, was able to give her some physical comforts, and introduced her to books and paintings. To lessen her loneliness, Christiane frequented local churches, where she studied the carved statues and stained glass windows. She copied illustrations from prayer books and the Bible. Even as a child, she found consolation in drawing. "I grew up in a world of adults. I had to be quiet, in a large house, and this restricted most other activities. With books, paper and crayon one could always create one's own world, which also defied intrusion by any unwanted people."

Born in Berlin in 1936, Christiane Pflug was only nine when the war finally ended. The years between were desolate. The fact that her affections were torn between her absent mother and her foster parent, left her inwardly insecure for the rest of her brief life. As a result, almost everything she later painted was pensively poetic. Hers was to be an in-looking art, emerging from deeply hidden feelings and a very restricted theme of the world to be seen through the window of the kitchen or bedroom. As she herself said in 1968, "I work in an enclosed and very private world."

Christiane remained in the Austrian Tyrol until she was twelve, after which she spent a few years with her mother in an apartment in Frankfurt. From the apartment window she sketched many views of a surrounding park, thus beginning her lifelong practice of depicting framed landscapes. After leaving school at fifteen, she went to live with her grandmother in Berlin, another adjustment for the child.

At seventeen Christiane decided to put her skill at drawing to practical use, and went to Paris to study fashion design. Paris brought the first real sunshine into her life. She disliked the dress designing course, but loved the city's light and buildings. "Paris is such a wonderful surrounding," she said. "It leads automatically to painting. Once I'd started, I felt this was for me."

Her desire to paint took on a new urgency a year later after she met her future husband, Michael Pflug, a medical student and artist, on a Paris-bound train. When he saw her drawings, Michael encouraged

On the Black Chair No. 2
Oil on canvas 1963 33 x 30
Collection: Mr Don Haig

On the Balcony No. 2
Oil on canvas 1963 52-1/2 x 39-1/2
Collection: Mrs J.H. Solway

Kitchen Door with Esther
Oil on canvas 1965 64 x 76
Estate of the Artist

Detail of *Kitchen Door with Esther*

her to paint, and during the summer of 1954, and on return trips to Paris during the next two years, Christiane did many paintings of the city. From the very beginning, she revealed a very original pictorial vision. Her tempera paintings of the Seine, of still lifes and buildings in Paris and Normandy were powerful personal statements for a self-taught eighteen-year-old girl. She found in painting a release from all the uprooted years of childhood, and she found in Michael Pflug someone who understood her creative needs. They were married in Munich in the summer of 1956.

The couple spent the next three years together in Tunisia, where Pflug went for his internship. They rented a studio-apartment in a six-hundred-year-old house in the centre of the Casbah at Tunis, and there their two daughters, Ursula and Esther, were born. In Africa Christiane painted a series of luminous and evocative still lifes and interiors, simple in theme but redolent with mood. Mostly temperas, these include *Still Life with Clock-face and Tiles* (1957), *Tunisian Interior* (1958) and *Bird Cage with Pears* (1958). The theme of the cage and dead birds appears in a number of her works, possibly symbolizing her own restricted childhood.

In the spring of 1959, when political violence grew in North Africa, Michael decided that it would be wise for Christiane to follow the example of her mother, now remarried, and go to Canada. He joined her here in 1960, but that first year alone with two children in a strange new environment was a cultural and emotional shock to Christiane. She settled into a suburb of Toronto – a dramatic contrast to the ancient *milieu* she had known in Tunis and Paris. The austere, hygienic high rises around her appeared at first as prisons. "I felt desperate," she later wrote, "and I felt I would never paint again." Slowly, she came to terms with the new setting, and from an apartment in an old house in downtown Toronto she began her first Canadian painting, of an adjacent railway yard. That work, in its simplicity, richness of mood and visual editing, foretold the remarkable cityscapes she was to achieve in the early 1970's. *Railway Yard in Rain* (1961 – Hart House, University of Toronto) and *Railway Yard in Winter* (1962) reflected her early creative adjustment to the local scene.

Toronto art dealer Avrom Isaacs saw Christiane's work when it was brought to his gallery for framing in 1961, and arranged an exhibition of her works in 1962. The exhibition consisted, for the most part, of drawings, though there were four small paintings of railway yards. The showing was a sell-out, which encouraged Christiane to embark on the series of large, major canvases upon which her reputation essentially rests.

In 1962 Christiane conceived her remarkable "doll" paintings, in which a great deal of symbolism relating to her own life may be found. *On the Black Chair No. 1*, *On the Black Chair No. 2*, *On the Balcony No. 2*, *Doll with Railway Yard* (Winnipeg Art Gallery) and *Under the Street Light* all date from that year. It is astonishing that these works, each a major achievement, could be produced in such a short time by a painter obliged also to carry out a domestic routine. She painted mostly in the kitchen and living room, in the morning hours and later at night when the children were asleep. It took her several months to complete each patiently composed work. She had to paint to live, and no obstacle seemed too great to keep her from her passion. The dolls she portrayed in these paintings are sadly haunting presences. In *On the Black Chair No. 2*, the tiny doll-child seems trapped within the embrace of dark wicker, the dying flowers in the background adding a note of despair. For Christiane, painting was a respite from a constantly recurring depression. "It is better to paint," she claimed, "than to worry about life."

Her dedication to her painting was absolute. "Painting dominates your life to the exclusion of everything," she said in an interview with Valerie Elliott in 1968. "You have to treat painting as a private part of your life, organize your life around it – but do not expect it to support you, because if you do, you have to compromise." Her approach to the act of painting was equally deliberate. She worked slowly. "It is hard to paint day after day for two months on one painting and keep the same strength of vision. There is a danger I will get tired, lapse into reproducing instead of really painting, putting dead paste on dead canvas instead of something that is really alive."

In 1965 Christiane began a number of canvases portraying her kitchen, with her children and the vista through the open kitchen door. These include the massive compositions, *Kitchen Door and Esther* (1965) and *Kitchen Door with Ursula* (1966 – Winnipeg Art Gallery). They took her seven and nine months, respectively, to complete, and are among her masterpieces. Rarely has a Canadian artist taken such routine material and created from it such compositions, combining ordered design and telling humanism. Here is the simplicity of the seventeenth-century Dutch Little Masters found on a large, contemporary scale, yet lacking neither intimacy nor magic. This is Christiane's world, her private kitchen preserve, expanded and full of mystery.

The Isaacs Gallery held a second exhibition of Christiane Pflug's work in 1964. Through it, her painting gained wider recognition, and she was honoured by three major public exhibitions within four years. In 1966 the Winnipeg Art Gallery gave her a retrospective show of

Cottingham School in Winter
Oil on canvas   1969-70   60 x 50
Estate of the Artist

Cottingham School with Black Flag
Oil on canvas 1971-72 56 x 54
Estate of the Artist

thirty-seven drawings and paintings. Three years later Hart House, University of Toronto, held a similar exhibition, and in 1971 the Sarnia Public Library and Art Gallery showed forty works done during the 1960's.

In the late 1960's the artist did her final series of canvases. She devoted most of her time to painting variations of a view to be seen from her third-floor studio room – a view that showed Cottingham School and the buildings beyond it. Between 1967 and 1972 she did eight variations on this simple theme. Though painted from nature, each represents a different mood and climate. In most, the Canadian flag undergoes colour changes from black to yellow, Like all of her major compositions, the Cottingham School paintings are executed on canvas in traditional oil colours, painted at an easel. They represent the most calculated design of all her works.

Christiane Pflug gave little concern to appearance. Toward the end of her life she usually wore faded jeans, a janitor's shirt, black leather coat and, always, workboots. She wore her dark auburn hair pulled back from a madonna-like face. She read Orwell, Dostoevsky and Thomas Wolfe, and included the brothers Le Nain, Ucello, Cranach and Seurat among her favourite painters – a reflection of her own classic, if unschooled, approach to art.

Christiane regularly suffered from severe depression, and towards the end of her life she tired easily, rarely wanting to leave her home. She began to speak of death as "a welcome sleep," and on April 4, 1972, at the age of thirty-five, she quietly committed suicide on the beach at Hanlan's Point, Toronto Island – one of her favourite painting places.

Christiane Pflug left behind a body of work which occupies a singular position in Canadian art. From an almost lifelong spiritual isolation, she brought forth poignant symbols of the twentieth-century's emotional malaise. Her work now hangs in such public collections as the National Gallery of Canada; The Winnipeg Art Gallery; Hart House, University of Toronto; and the Agnes Etherington Art Centre, Queen's University.

The Squirrel
Pencil 1968 12-1/2 x 10
Estate of the Artist

Christopher Pratt

Christopher Pratt is an ideal example of the true high realist; he has the ability to convert the regional into the universal. Like most realists, he prefers to create in the familiar environment of his youth, eliciting from it paintings that are classical and significant far beyond their immediate place of origin.

Pratt's roots in Newfoundland go back for several generations. His father and grandfather were born in the province, and his mother's family of Dawe have lived in the Bay Roberts area since the late 1700's. His great uncle, E.J. Pratt, one of Canada's greatest poets, came from Western Bay, Newfoundland.

Christopher was born in 1935 in St. John's, a city that, during his boyhood, was not exactly renowned for its interest in the arts. There was no local gallery, no professional artists, and virtually no books on art available. Fortunately, his paternal grandfather had begun painting watercolours as a hobby at sixty-five, and encouraged Christopher's interest. He gave him his first brushes and a book of instruction, *Painting in Watercolours,* by the American artist Adolf Dehn.

At seventeen, when he was in his last year at St. John's Prince of Wales Collegiate, Christopher began to make watercolours of local scenes and imaginary buildings. He painted things because he liked them and identified with them, not because he had any serious intention of becoming an artist. At that time, he says, he had never heard of Picasso, Matisse or any other major modern painter.

In the fall of 1952 Christopher enrolled at Memorial University in St. John's as an engineering student. But the more he painted the more uncertain he felt about his choice of a career. He was becoming increasingly serious about art, and in 1953 he decided to go to New Brunswick's Mount Allison University where a number of his friends had enrolled. "Unconsciously, I probably knew I was going to study Fine Art eventually," says Pratt, "but at the time I told my parents I wanted to study medicine. The fact that Mount Allison had a highly respected Fine Arts Department would merely be a plus." Having signed up for it, he did put in a year at Pre-Med, despite the fact that his watercolours had attracted the interest of his teachers. (Lawren P. Harris and Alex Colville were enthusiastic about his work, and Harris actually wrote a letter to Pratt's parents recommending that he study Fine Art.) But before his second year, Pratt decided he could no longer resist painting, and enrolled in the Fine Arts course.

Pratt admits that he took it easy at Mount Allison, spending much of his time doing props for events like the Junior Prom instead of class projects. He also found it very difficult to adjust to the discipline, and in the middle of his third year he dropped out. He returned to St.

Institution
Oil on masonite   1973   30 x 30
National Gallery of Canada

144

Shop on an Island
Oil on board 1969 33 x 36
Collection: Mr J.H. Moore

John's, determined to become an artist on his own, and for the next year and a half he returned to painting local watercolours, selling almost one a week, for prices ranging from $35 to $75. He concentrated on architectural themes, and his style gradually took on the bright, sharply rendered character which later became his stylistic trademark.

By the spring of 1957 Pratt felt the need to return to art school, and this time chose to go abroad. He applied by mail to a dozen different British art schools, finally deciding on Glasgow. He and a classmate, Mary West, married in September, before sailing for Scotland where they remained for two years.

Those years at the Glasgow School of Art brought the Canadian student the discipline and demanding training of which he was in need. Glasgow has long been known as the best provincial art school in Britain. It places great emphasis upon traditional fundamentals, and Pratt had to draw for three hours every morning from wooden geometric shapes before he was allowed to go on to draw from plaster casts. In the afternoons he took a general programme of sculpture, design, lettering, crafts and graphics. Each month there was an additional project for homework. The students were asked to illustrate a specified subject which could range from "People Making Beds" to "Cromwell Entering the Houses of Parliament." These works were then pinned up on the classroom wall and were scathingly criticized by the instructors, who made such remarks as "I could knit a better picture."

After their second year in Glasgow, Christopher and Mary began to feel homesick. They knew they wanted to make their home in Canada's Atlantic provinces eventually, and decided to do so right away.

In 1959, at the age of twenty-four, Pratt enrolled once more at Mount Allison, and this time completed his Bachelor of Fine Arts degree in two years. "At Mount Allison I was allowed to work completely on my own," he recalls. He set up his own studio in a small house rented from the university, and was only loosely involved in the academic programme, taking his work to instructors Alex Colville, Lawren P. Harris and Edward Pulford for criticism.

During his second year Pratt entered a painting in the Atlantic Art Awards sponsored by Dalhousie University, and won the second prize of $500 for an architectural painting, *Demolitions on the South Side* (1960). The scene represented an actual event the artist had witnessed in Sackville, and was based on more than a dozen memory drawings. He never draws his notes from the actual subject, just as his paintings of buildings are never literal representations. "Art is not objectivity," he says. "The actual object can be far too overwhelming. The last place

Young Woman with a Slip
Oil on board   1967   22-1/2 x 33-3/4
Private Collection

The Clothesline
Oil on board 1965 12 x 26
Collection Mr and Mrs F.J. Ryan

Detail of *Young Woman with a Slip*

I want to see when I am doing a painting is the place that inspired it."

After graduating from Mount Allison in 1961, Pratt joined the Extension Department of Memorial University, St. John's, with the dual responsibility of teaching adult art classes and arranging exhibitions for the University art gallery. During the more than two years he spent in teaching he managed to paint only one picture, *House and Barn*, which was purchased by Canada's External Affairs Department from the National Gallery's Biennial Exhibition of 1963. Frustrated by the lack of time to paint, he gave up his university post to devote his full time to art.

The Pratt family moved to St. Mary's Bay, fifty miles from St. John's, in May of 1963, and there they have lived ever since. The house is situated in 250 forested acres, within fifty feet of the Salmonier River, where salmon abound winter and summer. In this setting Christopher and Mary and their four children enjoy an eminently domestic life.

Pratt prefers to paint by artificial light and much of his work is done at night. His studio is a large room about twenty feet square, with high ceilings, bare white walls, and a gray floor – a decor in keeping with the subdued, almost monochrome character of the artist's paintings. No pictures hang on the studio walls; he does not like to have any of his completed works around, and ships them away or stores them out of sight as soon as they are finished.

Pratt's first works after moving to St. Mary's Bay were watercolours or drawings of architectural themes – old shops, closed places of business – representations of an idea rather than actual places. In the summer of 1964 he painted his first figure subject in oil, *Woman at a Dresser*. It was the beginning of a series of related compositions he was to produce during the next three years. He initially chose the figure, he says, because he "wanted to do some pieces that could not immediately and superficially be identified as being done in Newfoundland. I wanted to work in a genre that was more universal than Canadian geographic realism." As with his other figure works, the design concept and pose for *Woman at a Dresser* was completely worked out before he called in the model. The actual studies from the model were done in the evening, then later defined, after which the model was brought back a second time, and further definitions made. When in doubt, Pratt sticks with his original design concept, rather than adjust to the specific anatomy of the model, even if this means some distortion. "Sometimes," he says, "the point is reached where the live model is interfering with the design." Pratt invented the furniture in *Woman at a Dresser* and took the pattern on the wallpaper from an Eaton's mail order catalogue.

Woman at a Dresser was followed by *Young Girl with Sea Shells* (1953 –

Woman at a Dresser
Oil on board 1964 26-1/2 x 30-1/2
CIL Collection

150

Young Woman with a Slip
Pencil 1967 21 x 10-1/2
Memorial University, St. John's

Young Woman Dressing
Oil on board 1966 45 x 28
Collection: Mr J.K. Pratt

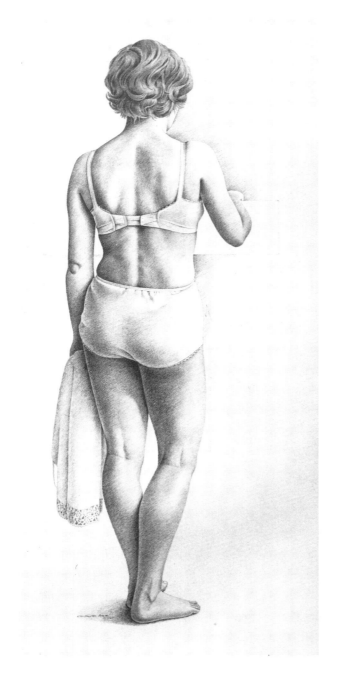

Memorial University of Newfoundland); *Woman at a Stove* (1965); his first nude – *Young Woman Dressing* (1966); and *Young Woman with a Slip* (1967). At that point, Pratt says, he got "figure indigestion" and returned to his architectural themes. He has not painted a figure subject since.

The architectural compositions are completely unpopulated; the presence of people is inferred rather than stated. This is ideally demonstrated in his *Three O'clock*. Pratt claims that in this picture he was not essentially painting the objects themselves but the mood of a time of day, the between-meals afternoon hours when all you can hear is the clock ticking. He wanted to recreate the personal associations with that mood. Like all of his paintings, *Three O'clock* is a composite. The genesis was the kitchen in his aunt's home at Bay Roberts where he went as a boy at Easter time. The actual stove was based on a sketch of one belonging to the postmistress at St. Mary's Bay. With Pratt the idea comes first, and the objects are used to give it pictorial form.

Night Window (1971) is a recreation in part of his grandfather's fireplace, and the blind and radiator, also reflected in the window, are separately existing objects, imagined or real. Pratt defines *Night Window*, with its reflections, as a "city picture," and says that most of the details for his art come from city or town architecture. The details of his painting *Institution* (1973) were checked out from the window of a Toronto hotel, and its conceptual origin, he feels, probably goes back to a childhood stay in a hospital from which he could see mainly chimney stacks and vents. *Window with Blind* (1970) had its beginnings when he woke up one morning facing a similar view in a Charlottetown hotel.

Since 1968 Pratt has concentrated on painting architectural forms. All of these, from *Shop on Sunday* (1968) to *Shop on an Island* (1969), *House in August* (1969) and *Institution*, are distilled studies of mood. Unlike his figure paintings, they are all rendered with a very limited colour palette of yellow ochre, cobalt blue, burnt sienna, alizarin crimson, ivory black and flake white. As in all of his work, the actual paint surface is invariably built up of small vertical brush strokes, usually on an acrylic-gessoed board or masonite.

Pratt deliberately elects not to use any story-telling devices in his paintings. Without them, he still manages to convey rich emotional feelings and ideas. His very disciplined reserve is actually the wellspring of his strength as an artist.

Fred Ross

The Maritime provinces in recent years have produced a number of Canada's best realist painters, and all of them, regardless of temptations to settle in more lucrative parts of the country, have chosen to remain near the communities in which they grew up. This is true of Alex Colville, Christopher Pratt and Tom Forrestall. New Brunswick painter Fred Ross is another who has displayed this tenacity and loyalty to the Atlantic homeland.

Ross was born just prior to the great depression, in 1927, and he grew up during a time when life on the east coast was very difficult, even more difficult than it was in the rest of Canada. There was no money for art, and the painters who persisted in creating did so in virtual poverty.

It was in such an atmosphere, with no illusions of great success, that Ross embarked upon a career in art. There was little of the *beaux-arts* glamour to be found in depressed Saint John. Only the example of two struggling local painters, Jack Humphrey and Miller Brittain, existed to inspire him. Only that and the art course offered by the Saint John Vocational School, which gave him an opportunity to learn the rudiments of drawing, design and painting.

Fred entered the Vocational School in 1942, at the age of fifteen. During his four years there he was notably encouraged by Ted Campbell, an instructor who had studied at the Art Institute of Chicago, a school known for its thoroughness of training. Campbell introduced his student to the fifteenth-century painters, Botticelli, Crivelli and Cosimo Tura, who appealed to the boy's natural leaning toward a linear kind of composition and rendering.

In the creative isolation of Saint John, young Ross was fortunate in finding a friend in Miller Brittain. He frequently visited the older artist's studio, where he gained much encouragement and advice. Brittain was a completely dedicated and disciplined painter, who during the depression years, and later as a war artist, created a number of remarkable portraits and figure studies in the classical tempera-oil techniques. Ross was also aware of Jack Humphrey's traditional studies painted throughout the 1930's and the early 1940's.

Fred Ross was thus thoroughly steeped in the art scene Saint John offered by the time he decided, a few years after graduation, to study mural painting in Mexico. He spent the summers of 1949 and 1950 in Mexico City, Taxco and San Miguel d'Allende. In Mexico City he met one of his favourite artists, Diego Rivera, and did several drawings of the great muralist working on his famous designs for the National Palace. His encounter with Rivera further heightened the young Canadian's ambition to do wall paintings, and he travelled south to Taxco,

The Red Skirt
Casein tempera 1972 Diameter 30-1/2
Gallery Dresdnere

Girl on a Rocking Horse
Casein tempera 1971 30 x 24
Gallery Dresdnere

The Card Game
Casein tempera 1973 36 x 24
Gallery Dresdnere

156

where he joined the workshop of noted Mexican-American painter, Patrick O'Higgins. Through O'Higgins, he obtained a commission to design a mural for the local Hotel de la Borda. Working freely on a large scale, to a carefully co-ordinated design, was an invaluable experience for Ross, which he was to put to use later in a series of murals in the Maritimes.

For any artist, especially one in his early twenties, the Maritimes was a difficult place just after the war. Virtually no paintings were being purchased, and the only way a painter could survive was by teaching. Upon his return from Mexico, therefore, Ross joined his old school, Saint John Vocational. He was a part-time teacher there for many years, becoming supervisor of its art department from 1966 until 1970, when he retired from teaching to paint full time.

Ross' studies in Mexico had virtually no influence upon his style or subject matter. He continued to paint compositions in the manner of the fifteenth-century Italian masters, particularly the Ferrarese genius, Cosimo Tura. Ross was fascinated by Tura's crimpled handling of drapery and his sober-visaged sitters. The resulting tempera panels, featuring Harlequins, masked lovers, fluted columns, lutes and draped skulls, seem a far romantic remove from the stark, hilly harbour city of Saint John. Their symbolism and highly decorative manner related much more to the classic European scenes which Ross managed to survey in four annual trips commencing in 1952. These were the years when his neo-Italian style was at its most eclectic, resulting in such large, ambitious compositions as *Seated Harlequin* (1952) and *Harlequin and Four Dancers* (1955). Exotic Renaissance concept and Maritime practicality are typically joined in the latter work. At the time it was painted, Ross and his wife, Sheila, were living in an old house that had been built by a sea captain, and all the picture's details of ornate columns and throne were copied from the decorations in their Saint John rooms.

A portrait of his wife, *Sheila in Blue* (1955 – Beaverbrook Art Gallery, Fredericton), was the first painting by Ross to be included in a public collection. Sheila had originally come to Saint John from England to teach ballet, and since their marriage in 1954, inspired by visits to her dancing school, he has done many ballet studies. His teen-age daughters, Lorna and Kathleen, have modelled for most of these works.

In 1955, Ross was included in the National Gallery exhibition, *Five Maritime Painters,* which introduced his work to a larger Canadian audience for the first time. It also revealed his continuing struggle to integrate a very contemporary scene with a Renaissance compositional approach. The National Gallery show included *Boys in a Graveyard*

Marsh Hawk
Casein tempera 1971 36 x 25
Collection: Dr and Mrs Kornberg

Young Girl Resting
Casein tempera 1970 Diameter 48
Gallery Dresdnere

which brings together two teen-aged boys in running shoes, surrounded by ancient wrought iron enclosed sarcophagi and obelisks. At the same time, a number of portraits of modern "leather jacket boys," *Portrait of Vernon* (1956), *Boy with Monkey* (1956), and *Boy with Broken Arm* (1956) were shown at the Greenwich Gallery in 1956. These are evocative, moody studies of high school boys in their most casual dress. In depicting the texture of leather and fur trim, the artist has attempted to bring Renaissance portraiture up to date.

Ross' work in recent years has been progressively less decorative and devoid of the earlier romantic props. His compositions have become more open, and his drawing highly selective and simplified. By the time of his one-man exhibition at Charlottetown's Confederation Centre Art Gallery, in 1970, he had completely absorbed his earlier Renaissance studies, and entered into a totally contemporary creative area. Modern French painter Jean Balthus had joined Cosimo Tura as a major influence. Balthus inspired a series of paintings based on Ross' daughters, including *Girl with Mirror* (1968-70), *Young Girl Resting* (1970) and *The Red Shirt* (1972). Each of these illustrates the artist's belief that he can heighten the psychological intensity of his concepts by concentrating upon the single figure.

Ross now lives in Saint John, with his wife, two daughters and son Christopher. His studio in the city centre, formerly a photographer's, includes two large rooms forty by twenty feet in size.

For many years Ross has followed the same painting methods. He does a complete preparatory drawing in pencil, which is then transferred onto a masonite panel covered with a gesso ground. Upon this, he works directly in casein colours. The resulting pictures have been shown in a number of major one-man shows in recent years – New Brunswick Museum (1965, '71), University of New Brunswick (1965, '71), Walter Klinkhoff Gallery, Montreal (1971), Memorial University, St. John's (1965), Mount Allison University (1970) and Gallery Dresdnere, Toronto (1973).

Jeremy Smith

Jeremy Smith, at half the age, or less, of such realist pioneers as Alex Colville, E.J. Hughes and Ernest Lindner, represents the young artists who are bringing fresh techniques and imagination to the richly varied sum of realism in Canada.

Jeremy was born in Louth, Lincolnshire, in 1946, but grew up in the heart of Toronto's downtown Yorkville district, a complex of art galleries, boutiques, cafés and little residential side streets. It was on one of these side streets, Scollard, that Jeremy lived as a boy with his parents, older sister and younger brother. Their backyard faced Jesse Ketchum School, which he attended until he was thirteen. Jesse Ketchum has a rough-and-tumble reputation, where an involvement in sports is almost a necessity, and young Jeremy, who later played three years for the noted Marlboro Juniors, was involved in hockey from an early age.

Sports found a balance in art. From the age of eight, Jeremy used astronomical photographs to draw views of the heavens in pencil and blue ink – an interest he caught from his father, a former Royal Air Force officer who was a radar electronics expert and amateur astronomer. Astronomy brought Jeremy his first art commission at the age of eleven. He did an oil painting of a space station, for which he received thirty dollars.

Jeremy's big-city boyhood had definite advantages for someone interested in art. He delivered for the neighbourhood fish and chip shop on Saturdays, but he could spend Sunday afternoons at the Royal Ontario Museum, where he had ready access to natural and man-made forms ranging from dinosaurs to Tang pottery. Frequently he visited the many private galleries in Toronto's Yorkville area.

At sixteen Jeremy spent eight weeks in hospital as a result of a hockey accident. The injury ended his ambitions to be a future professional hockey player, but gave him more time to paint. He worked constantly at his art in his spare time, purchasing his supplies by working at a local supermarket. He also spent a good deal of time analyzing the exhibits that were held in local private galleries. Two artists who impressed him were Zao-Wou-Ki, a Chinese abstract painter, and Jack Chambers, whose work first introduced him to high realism. Jeremy readily admits that Zao-Wou-Ki was the key to his early financial success at painting. From the age of fifteen he did his own six-foot versions of the Chinese artist's abstract style, and started selling them. They sold readily, and he probably had the highest income of any student at Jarvis Collegiate. In his teens he made as much as $2,500 a year painting in his spare time. He bought a motorcycle and started a collection of art books.

Surprise
Egg tempera on board 1972 30 x 36
Collection: Mr Gerry Clark

Arrival
Egg tempera on board 1971-72 36 x 47
Private Collection

Detail of *Arrival*

Study of a Child
Sumi ink on paper 1972 32-1/2 x 24
Marlborough Godard Gallery

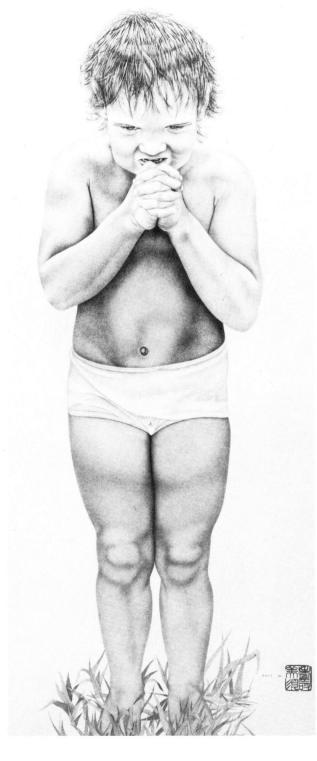

When he was seventeen, Jeremy took a folio of his work into the Canada High Arts Foundation which concerned itself with secondary school art, and was accepted for showing there. The Foundation sold his works regularly for $150 each, among them figurative drawings which were gradually taking priority for him over his earlier fashionable abstracts. In 1964 the High Arts Foundation included two of Smith's pen-and-ink studies in a show sent to Canada's Tokyo Embassy. It was his first contact with Japan, a country which was later to have a vital impact on his career.

During his last year at Jarvis Collegiate, in 1965, Jeremy spent some of the money he had earned on a three-month summer trip to Europe, where he visited galleries in England, France, Italy, Switzerland and Germany. It was strictly a period of absorption, and he did no actual drawing or painting. Despite his early success, he was still not committed to art as a lifetime career, and on his return to Canada he enrolled at the University of Western Ontario, intending to graduate in Philosophy.

The summer after his first university year he worked as a host for the Ontario Pavilion at Montreal's Expo 67. While there, he also completed a book of drawings of the various international pavilions. During his second year at Western he enrolled in the university's fledgling Fine Arts course, but although he did well academically, found the art course monotonous and restricting. This was his only exposure to formal art teaching, and his third year was spent in Philosophy and French Literature.

Despite his disinterest in formal art instruction, Smith was busy creatively during his university years. He did pastel portraits of his fellow students, and was given two one-man shows of realist drawings at the University of Toronto's Trinity College "Buttery" in 1965 and 1969. One of his drawings was bought by Toronto dealer Simon Dresdnere, who was later to represent him.

After graduating from Western in 1969, Smith was employed for three summer months creating display graphics for a Mid-Canada Development Conference held at Lakehead University in Thunder Bay. On his return to Toronto he was accepted as a host for the Canadian Pavilion at Osaka's Expo 70, and after studying Japanese for five months, left for Japan in February 1970.

His stay in Osaka had a cardinal influence on the twenty-four-year-old Smith. He found Japanese art and painting materials a special revelation, and it finally decided him to become a full-time painter. He remained in Japan for a full year, the first six months employed at the Osaka fair. On side trips to museums, he was impressed by the works of

Sleeping Boy
Sumi ink on paper   1970   12-1/4 x 16
Collection: T. Lempicki

Study of Dogs
Sumi ink on paper   1972   25-1/4 x 34-3/4
Marlborough Godard Gallery

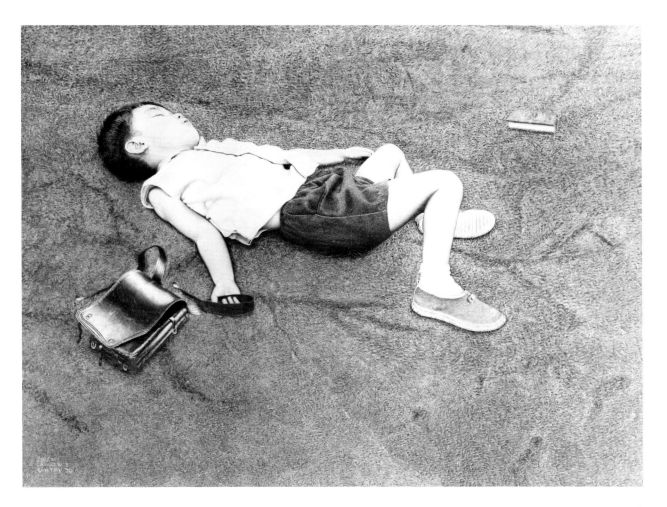

such Oriental masters as Korin, Hokusai and Sotatsu. He was determined this was the way he wanted to paint, bringing together careful design and consummate detail. He bought books on Japanese art, rice paper, sumi ink and fine bamboo-handled brushes. At nights, after his day at the Canadian Pavilion, he practised doing calligraphy exercises, and learned the character of his new materials. He also sketched at the Kabuki theatre and did drawings of children in a schoolyard near the international community where Expo employees were housed.

Smith found that the delicate line drawing obtainable with the Japanese brushes fulfilled his realist inclinations, and he began a small series of highly finished sumi-ink drawings on heavy, smooth Japanese paper. In the six months after his Expo duties ended in Osaka he completed five small paintings, each requiring one month. Among these were *Sleeping Boy,* in which the details of texture, such as the scratches on the subject's schoolbag, became almost microscopic and impossible to reproduce. When he returned to Toronto early in 1971, Smith showed these drawings to Simon Dresdnere who displayed and sold a number of them. It was his first representation by a major gallery.

Smith's first large work after his return was a portrait of his brother, which took three months to complete, in a mixture of egg tempera and sumi ink. He was dissatisfied with it, and began an even more ambitious composition, *Arrival,* in October 1971. *Arrival* portrays the artist with his fiancée (now his wife), Magda Seydegart, sitting on a wharf overlooking Lake Joseph in northern Ontario. The subject developed, he says, "because there was always someone arriving from across the water. The only way to reach the point we were at was by boat, yet in late August we were rarely alone." Smith's compositions are very carefully designed, and *Arrival* is based on a series of basic triangular motifs, carefully repeated. Perspective, as in Japanese art, is distorted to suit the artist's whim.

Like all of Smith's major works, *Arrival* is painted on a heavy handmade paper board, glued on to either masonite panel or plywood. He paints in several layers, building up an initial coat in egg tempera, then drawing over it in sumi ink and finishing up with a second coat of egg tempera. Generally, he works from light to dark, and each small area of the painting is completed before he moves on to the next. As he approaches each untouched white area, he "finds as he goes." In this way, Smith completed *Arrival* in just under six months.

Surprise, which took three months, portrays the niece of a friend with the artist's dog Peppy, in a studio room used by Smith in 1972. Its quiet, deliberate, vertical and horizontal space design is in strong contrast to the angles which dominate *Arrival.* After *Surprise,* Smith embarked upon a tribute to one of his favourite European painters, Pieter Brueghel the Elder, by doing his contemporary version of that sixteenth-century Flemish master's *Children's Games.* He first did many individual studies of children playing in a schoolyard where his brother worked in Toronto's east end. After planning the basic composition and placing the scene in the same Lake Joseph locale as *Arrival,* Smith flew to Vienna to re-acquaint himself with the original in the Kunsthistorisches Museum. He began the painting in August 1972, and completed it eight months later. The picture contains a multitude of minor symbols, but basically, Smith says, he wanted to capture the transience of man's activities against the permanence of earth, water and sky. Certainly *Children's Games* is one of the most ambitious figure compositions ever attempted by a Canadian painter. It contains 165 figures (as against Brueghel's 80), each one carefully conceived and rendered. It bears out Smith's contention, and that of many high realists, that formal training is not the only route to creative success. Natural talent, determination and originality of vision can lead a self-taught painter to achievements far beyond most art college graduates.

Children's Games
Egg tempera on board 1972-73 29-1/2 x 46
Marlborough Godard Gallery

Photo Credits

Tom Moore: 15, 89, 113, 118, 119, 121, 124 (top), 127, 129, 133, 134, 153, 154, 158, 161, 162, 163, 165, 168
Ken Barton: 77, 79, 81, 82, 83, 85, 86, 87
Ron Vickers: 41, 42, 43, 45, 46, 49
National Gallery of Canada: 11, 27, 28, 35, 37, 63, 69, 72, 108, 115, 116, 143
Fischer Fine Arts: 65, 75
Eberhard Otto: 53, 54, 57, 58, 59, 135, 138, 139
Marlborough Godard: 144, 146, 147, 150 (right)
ADS: 90, 92, 93, 96, 97
Dominion Gallery: 107, 109, 111
Lesser Studio: 123
TDF: 58, 68
Kanute Javer: 124 (bottom)
Gabor Szilasi: 71
Art Gallery of Ontario: 19 (bottom)
Jennifer Harper: 149
Lloyd Bloom: 20, 25
Joseph Klima Jr: 19 (top)

Index of Reproductions

Index

This book was designed by Hugh Michaelson and
filmset in 11 pt. Baskerville by Qualitype Company.
Colour separations are by Graphic Litho-Plate Limited.
Printed by Sampson Matthews Ltd. on
200M Lustercoat Enamel and bound by
T. H. Best Printing Company Limited.